C000031155

How t

Sales Funnel

What the Leaders in Your Industry Are Doing To Stay At the Top

By

Omid Kazravan

professional advice. The content within this book has been derived from various sources. Please consult a licensed professional before attempting any techniques outlined in this book.

By reading this document, the reader agrees that under no circumstances is the author responsible for any losses, direct or indirect, which are incurred as a result of the use of information contained within this document, including, but not limited to, — errors, omissions, or inaccuracies.

Table of Contents

How to Build an Online Empire from Scratch x

Introduction 11

Chapter 1: The ABM Mindset You Need For This Book 13

What Is ABM Anyway? 13

Chapter 2: The Goals You Can Set In ABM Marketing...20

Set Realistic Goals That You Can Achieve 21

Roles Assigning and Alignment 22

Define Your Targets 22

Developing Your Persona.....................................23

Mapping Everything 23

Create Actionable Content....................................24

How Are You Going To Engage Your Audience? 24

Perform Analysis of Vital Data 25

Chapter 3: What Is A Sales Funnel and Why Do You Need One? 27

Understanding the Sales Funnel Stages 28

Why You Need A Sales Funnel for Your Business 30

In Conclusion...34

Chapter 4: The Purpose of a Strong Pipeline 35

Tips on Strong Pipeline Construction....................36

A Strong Pipeline Needs Email Marketing............39

Email Marketing Needs an Email List 39

Chapter 5: Know Your Target Audience and Qualify Your Prospects.. 41

Identifying and Analyzing Your Target Market.... 42

Conclusion.. 46

Chapter 6: Building Your Buyers Persona 47

Defining the Buyer's Persona 47

Why Are Buyer Personas Important?..................... 48

Personas Will Evolve and Change 49

How to Create Buyer Personas............................... 49

Finding Interviewees to Help You Research Your Buyer Persona.. 50

Tips for Recruiting Interviewees 53

Twenty Questions to Ask In Persona Interviews .. 54

Identifying the Number of People to Interview..... 57

How to Use Your Research to Create Your Persona 57

Conclusion.. 59

Chapter 7: The Lead Magnet.................................. 60

Lead Magnet Definition 61

Lead Magnet Purpose 62

Creating a Lead Magnet?.. 62

Promoting Your Lead Magnet................................. 67

Where Else Can You Use A Lead Magnet? 70

It's Time to Do It... 71

Chapter 8: Creating a Great Landing Page..........**72**

What Is A Landing Page? 73

Advantages of an Effective Landing Page.............74

Considerations before Making a Landing Page 75

How to Make Great Landing Pages.......................77

Chapter 9: Giving an Upset Offer on the Back End
....**82**

What Is Customer Service?...................................82

Skills to Improve Your Customer Service.............83

Offering A Downsize Option.................................90

Conclusion 91

Chapter 10: Split Testing..**92**

Split Test Definition...92

Who Split Testing Is Right For..............................93

Why Should You Run a Split Test?.......................94

Preparing For Your First Split Test 95

Using ClickFunnels for Split Testing 97

Conclusion 97

Chapter 11: Call to Actions **99**

The Basics of Call to Action.................................99

Guide to Building an Effective Call to Action 100

Additional Call to Action Best Practices 104

Chapter 12: Plan for Generating Traffic **105**

How Has This Happened? 105

Benefits of Facebook Marketing for a Business..106

Conclusion 110

Chapter 13: Why Paid Traffic Is King 111

Google AdWords 112

Facebook Adverts 114

LinkedIn Adverts 115

Twitter Adverts 116

Concluding the Chapter 118

Chapter 14: Why Your Fear of Spending Money on Marketing Is False 119

Why Do You Need To Spend Money On Marketing? 122

Concluding the Chapter 124

Chapter 15: Running Facebook Ads 125

How to Run Facebook Ads 126

Chapter 16: Email Lists and Why You Need One 135

What an Email List Entails 136

Why Small Businesses Need To Grow Their Email List 137

Why You Need To Grow Your Email List 138

You Can Do More with an Email List 139

Tips on Building Your Email List 140

Concluding the Chapter 142

Chapter 17: Email Drip Campaigns and How to Build Them 143

How to Set Up a Drip Campaign 144

Concluding the Chapter 148

Chapter 18: Plan on Engaging Your Audience ..149

How to Boost Engagement 149

Chapter 19: Build Relationships 156

Stage 1: Awareness..157

Stage 2: Achieving interest and Evaluation.........158

Stage 3: Gaining Trust 158

Stage 4: Action...159

Managing Sales Funnel like a Guru.....................160

Concluding the chapter 161

Chapter 20: Become an Authority in Your Area163

What Is The Authority Principle?.........................163

How You Can Become an Authority....................164

Concluding the Chapter 168

Chapter 21: Convert Your Leads 169

How to Convert Leads Into Sales 169

Concluding the Chapter 174

Chapter 22: You Need a System for Your Sales Funnel 175

What Makes A Sales Funnel Different From Your Website?...175

Reasons Why You Need a Sales Funnel System .177

Conclusion: All the Funnel Websites and Why I Believe ClickFunnels Is the Best and Most Robust One...**180**

ClickFunnels Overview 182

How to Build an Online Empire from Scratch...187

References **188**

How to Build an Online Empire from Scratch

Before we begin I have a free gift for you from Russell Brunson - for those of you that don't know Russell Brunson is, he's the man that created Click Funnels. In my opinion it's the best funnel website out there and it has also helped create the most millionaires. If you're reading this book, then you want to be the best in your industry. This book will give you the play by play to have people PAYING you for your advice. I am able to give you his best selling book for free right down here. I only have a few copies left so please get them while you can. Just click this http://bit.ly/giftfunnelbook

Introduction

Thank you for taking the time to purchase this book and getting to read it. It means that you have been looking for a solution to a problem that you don't know what to do about – increasing your sales online. We suffered the same until I found what it means by having a sales funnel and what it can do for your business. Here is a short story about what made me write this book.

I was selling t-shirts online through Amazon, and I was also helping a friend of mine sell his short eBook about how to build a solar panel on an RV. The problem I had on Amazon was that if I did not have any t-shirts to sell, that's it, and my friend's book was not doing so well. We sat down and decided to design a website that would help us sell the t-shirts. After two months of hiring a designer and doing everything we needed for the website, it was time to upload the pictures and sell.

After about three weeks, I noticed something was wrong with the site. Nothing was selling. After spending thousands of dollars on it, nothing was happening. That was the end of everything. With no job to do and no sales, I was in a dark corner.

Later, a friend came to me and over a cup of coffee, he mentioned something to with sales funnels. In particular, he was talking about building a funnel with ClickFunnels. I thought it was a good idea to try as nothing else was working. I sat down after that with my computer and researched about ClickFunnels on the internet. They had everything that I wanted to hear, but for me to verify, I had to try.

After 48 hours of building a small site on the platform which was under a free subscription for 14 days and pushing traffic for the t-shirts, I made sales that were enough to pay for my six months' subscription. Each month was costing me $97 to keep the funnel going on.

Now, I know you are trying to think of how I did it. This book will explain all the things that you have to consider if you want to build a successful sales funnel. Unlike me who had to learn as I progressed, you will have all the tips with you as you build your online business and try to convert potential prospects into customers. I have talked about all the fundamental points which I have, structured into chapters. By the end of this book, you will know why you need to start building your sales funnel and why ClickFunnels is one of the best platforms to join.

Chapter 1: The ABM Mindset You Need For This Book

Before we venture entirely into sales funnel creation and implementation, let us first look at what is helping us do it in the first place – the idea of Account-Based Marketing (ABM). If you are leading an online business, this is something that you may have heard or see without actually knowing what it is. If you are reading about ABM for the first time, let me tell you that it has been around for as early as 2003.

It is a hot topic that is trending in the e-commerce world but much time has passed since the ideology was introduced. Most of the CMO's in the B2B marketing are considering it if it is not their number one priority.

However, even those who understand it well will have different definitions of what it is.

What Is ABM Anyway?

If we put it in a way that you can comprehend what it is all about, it is a technique that controls all the marketing gear to do one thing – engage the targeted accounts to become buyers. Remember that we need to sell our products and services here. What ABM does is to force the marketing and sales departments to work together based on the messages sent to specific accounts.

What is the aim here? To increase revenues within a short time, with all resources controlled under one roof. That is what a platform like ClickFunnels is doing to every successful entrepreneur who has joined.

Now, instead of using your lead generation efforts to chase a wide array of customers, what the marketing team will focus on here is the ABM and what the sales are reflecting (Rietkerk, 2019). That way, you can pick the crucial prospects that can later aid in tailoring your messages and programs for the buyers in the targeted accounts.

Getting the idea of what it is all about so that you can have the mindset is one thing; the next one is what you need to know about ABM. Many marketers who still cannot get it would love to see it go away. But with AI being around, such a phenomenon in creation is here to stay.

Since we are concentrating all the marketing forces on specific accounts, does it mean we disregard what lead generation has been doing before ABM came knocking? What will it take to leave out everything else you know before reaping the rewards?

I once had a round table with some of the ABM gurus,

and this was an issue that took the whole session by storm. There were concerns about how you go about it on your way to success. Here is what they had to share with other marketers in the forum. As you read through the rest of this book, the points below are what you are going to use to guide you in the right direction.

Every business is different out there. For you to stay at the top, it is crucial not to let fear rule out the possibility of learning something new.

ABM Is Not the Sole Solution to All Your Marketing Problems

If it is a technique that is making your competitors outrun you, don't think it is the one bullet you have been looking for all this time (Pike, 2016). It is much better when you see it as a quick solution to your marketing and selling but what will make you understand better is thinking about it as a new philosophy. It's another way of driving your organization or idea of what matters the most – the interested customer accounts.

It's Vital to Fasten the Organizational Buy-In

You need to focus on more than what the sales and marketing aspects are doing. That means considering the external messages, pre-sales, after-sale support, and overall customer experience too. Everything and everyone involved needs to dedicate towards knowing which the right target accounts are and those involved. Next is all about the value propositions and the messages you need to use to engage them.

That way, you will be concentrating on the contacts you get from one customer account area and seeing if there are new opportunities to explore or new connections to call and cross-sell. If your team is not venturing into effective communication, customers will never get the vital information they are looking for before engaging in the buying process.

ABM Is a Winner in Aligning Sales and Marketing

By understanding ABM, you agree that it brings a perfect alignment between marketing and the sales generated. That means if you have people in your team who are always aiming the target markets and react by how sales are performing, it will be difficult to convince them about going the ABM way if they find it as a distraction to their methods.

It is better when you surround yourself with visionary people who can see what your new approach can do.

Big Organizations Will Find It Hard Joining A ClickFunnels Platform than the Small to Mid-Level Businesses

If you are finding it hard to market, all by yourself with all the marketing resources you need, getting into a platform that can solve that will be an easy decision. However, for big organizations, who are already succeeding in what they do, it is going to be tricky when they learn that it is possible to abandon most of what they believe in to simplify market and sell before collecting the reports.

On the other hand, you can introduce the idea to the company by aiming at those individuals that play a strategic role. They are the ones who can view the long-term goal and see you through the cause.

The Customer Is King Here – Know Them Well

Every department involved should be tailored towards knowing everything about the customers. That means even considering the sales-side reports. According to one of the attendees at the round table, you need a personalization approach that requires thorough follow up and investigation. The marketing and sales aspects need to look for more information about their customers by, for example, digging more on social media after checking the individual buyer accounts.

After Target Identification, Avoid Overloading Clients with Information

It is a common tendency that after identifying the right individuals, you get tempted to push every other detail you think is necessary to them. In the end, clients get more than what they require which makes them lose interest due to you pushing vehemently for your products or services. What you give them should be sieved by timing, knowing what they have seen, and answering what they are looking for.

Data Is Vital In Your ABM Strategy

Different forms of data are confusing many marketers especially if you are working for a big company. If you have a tool that will help you arrange and clean the data before disposing it to customers, then you can concentrate more on the personal research that will help you build a rich data set for your ABM protocol. ClickFunnels is one place that can help you arrange your data collection as you check through what you need to deliver.

Before we look at the goals you can set as you build a sales funnel, it is essential to keep the above points in mind. Account-based marketing will involve concentrating your resources on specific buying accounts and giving the right information that will trigger sales and after sales reports that will lead to further engagement. Therefore, you need to know where you lie before going all in to make the fortunes.

Chapter 2: The Goals You Can Set In

ABM Marketing

Are you an online marketer or aspiring to be one? The words "Account Based Marketing" will be one of the things you will often be hearing. You may have subscribed to a couple of email newsletters that have already shown you how ABM can be great for your business. Since the companies involved need to create customers that will bring in the relevant revenue, it makes sense to join a platform like ClickFunnels or something similar to help you aim your marketing efforts at organizations that agree with your target customer profiling.

On the other hand, knowing that it is the best thing to do for your business and actualizing it are two distant relatives (Burton, 2017). You need to apply the theory derived into how ABM can be used to reach the appropriate customers. You need a contingency plan that everyone involved can follow.

Before you join an ABM platform as I did with ClickFunnels, it is crucial that you lay out some goals to be achieved in the course of taking your entrepreneurship to the next level.

Set Realistic Goals That You Can Achieve

One thing that I have realized as I practiced ABM is that you need clearly-defined goals. Otherwise, you will be facing issues in the business that need quick adjustments, and if you are not fast enough, the brand can stagnate. As a marketer, your goals should pave the way towards incremental growth as you aim to reach beyond the value set for new business leads.

Consider the number of customers that your marketing efforts are expected to bring in and serve in a specific period. How many leads does your sales team need for them to uncover new opportunities? What is the amount of new business that you marketers are expected to steer?

You may be having the relevant data to create a waterfall model that will reveal the ideal market-driven pipeline. Some programs follow such a model and offer helpful tips on how to go about it. If you don't have enough information to make the plan, check your competitors and other industry standards to determine your leads.

After that, you can go back to your data and adjust accordingly over time.

Roles Assigning and Alignment

When you look at ABM marketing, the sales and marketing departments must work together for the betterment of the program. As you make your plan in the step above, make sure to define the roles of each participant in the arrangement. According to statistics, companies are more than 60% better at achieving more business deals when the sales and marketing staff work together.

Define Your Targets

As you start, you might tend to think that declaring your target accounts is the first thing to do and it's what will set your business struggle free. Target account identification is what you need, but it is only a small part in your whole strategy.

ClickFunnels can help you create an account list based on the information to feed on your end. As you go about defining your target, here are some of the things to consider despite the platform you are using:

- The character you are looking for in the best companies. Which companies suit your character description?

- Are there potential opportunities waiting for exploitation in the sales pipeline?

- Which corporations or organizations are visiting your site or using your content and are ready to involve you as part of a solution?

- Do you have any connects to companies via known advocates or partners?

Developing Your Persona

As long as you will be operating in an ABM guided strategy, you should know one thing: companies do not buy, people do. Knowing your target companies is super okay, but people are the ones to buy your products and services, so they become the source of income. If you don't have a buyer's persona already, we will cover that in detail in chapter 6.

Mapping Everything

Once you get the target account lists and the personas in those accounts, you realize the specific persons that you would like to connect within each company. Do you have a CRM (Customer Relationship

Management) program? It could be a single program or a module integrated into your ABM platform. Get the data from your target accounts and feed it in there. When new leads come by, match them with the accounts set in the CRM. It can take some time, but the fruits are sweeter.

Create Actionable Content

Content that you deliver through your marketing efforts is the most vital aspect of B2B marketing today. The sad thing today is that the marketing automation protocol gives a one-to-many form of communication. Most people out there will filter easily anything that comes from the machine's result. Having more personalized content for your customers like what ClickFunnel helps marketers to will give you a better chance of raising your awareness creation.

How Are You Going To Engage Your Audience?

ClickFunnels always show ideas on how to actively engage your audience. The message here is that once you get your account lists, strategy on content, and the set persona, you now need marketing techniques that will allow active audience engagement. While most of us will focus on inbound marketing, which is crucial, not all the prospects you target will respond to your call. For you to reach the set goals, there is a need to consider the outbound marketing approach which may include ad-targeting strategies and third-party marketing content abilities among others. Remember to do that on the targeted accounts only.

Perform Analysis of Vital Data

ABM is known to bring in tremendous results. Companies who have already engaged see that it is something that can generate more than 200% revenue once you concentrate on the targeted marketing efforts. However, to achieve this, you cannot view ABM as something you will set and forget about it.

It will take some time for you to have the revenue data needed to steer your success. For the first 4-6 months, you can start by evaluating the engagement in your personas. Do you have the right people within your targets to use your content? As you go on, start now to look at your revenue status and if it reflects on your marketing efforts via the ABM program.

ClickFunnels can help you with data collection

mechanisms that will aid you in performing a detailed analysis of what is going on.

As we conclude, the above are goals that will propagate your journey in becoming a successful online business person as you build your sales funnel.

Chapter 3: What Is A Sales Funnel and Why Do You Need One?

I do mention sales funnels regularly in my one on one meetings, and also you may have come across these words while going through my written content. So, now I want to emphatically untangle what sales funnels are for those who have never heard of them to comprehend quickly. In today's world, when I go through websites, what I notice is that what most upcoming enterprisers lack in these business websites is sensible sales funnels. I am not castigating or denouncing anyone's business site; it is just that lack of a substantial, influential, and far-reaching sales funnel which, in this case, is your website can discredit your online legacy and lower your products' sales. This can make your efforts and resources in building the site go to waste. Sales funnels are here to salvage your online legacy. So, below is an introductory part of what they are. In the end, you have a clear definition of what sales funnels are.

If you want to try Clickfunnels here is a free 14 day trial that you can have full access to
http://bit.ly/Omidsfreetrial

Understanding the Sales Funnel Stages

In ClickFunnels, there are sales funnels which are meant to rescue your online legacy in five main significant stages, from the first time you have a potential client visit your website to the time he or she buys your product. In your business, you are allowed to develop as many stages as you would like to, but the ones below are the essential ones;

- *Awareness:* This is the stage when a potential client visits your website via an ad, Google, or any other social media platform like Facebook, Instagram, or Twitter and discovers the product you are selling. They notice that your product can solve a problem that they may be having or experiencing.

- *Interest:* The second stage is when a potential client starts looking at how to achieve a particular objective. He or she may research for answers on Google, and this is the time that you interest him or her with fascinating and catchy information about what you would like to offer. This is when he or she may show interest in your product and signs up.

- *Decision:* This is the stage where the client looks for authenticity in your product like looking for how you brand it or how you uniquely package it to make a purchase. He or she may now want to exploit your solution. At this step, an offer is made by maybe use of a sale page, a call, a webinar, a message, or something else.

- *Action:* In this step, the client is making a final decision, signing your contract, and buying your product. The payment then immediately reflects on your account. Notably, in this stage, you may notice more costs on your sales funnels. Not all communications with a potential client lead to a successful purchase. But with ClickFunnels, you are assured of high sales.

- *Retention:* The last stage is when the client has joined your organization. Loyal, contented, and satisfied clients now promote your products by use of the word of mouth which is the best mode of advertising to increase your online sales. This helps you acquire more clients with time. You can now ensure repetitive business with this client by warmly treating him or her with things like more information about what you have added or something you would like them to know. You can offer them the following:

- o Unique offers

- o Follow-ups

- o Product manuals

- o High-tech assistance

- o Emails

The above steps show how sales funnel for any enterpriser are convenient to use in one's enterprise website since they initiate a very long-lasting relationship between you and your clients.

Why You Need A Sales Funnel for Your Business

Consumers Are Sophisticated

In today's world, clients do a lot of in-depth analysis before buying a product. This is unlike long ago. Now people have the internet to research anything. They want and have an urge to know what difference your product has and why it is worth their money because nobody wants to waste their funds. They will prefer buying a product from an enterprise they have confidence in, mostly an enterprise they have heard about from a friend or previously purchased from

(Velji, 2018). As a copywriter, I get paid a lot of money to work on these pages, and from experience, I can freely tell you that cold selling ad traffic only gives you insignificant results. The numbers in sales will continue to decrease since it is not efficient. A sales funnel equips you with the ability to get clients. ClickFunnels enable you to understand today's cultured clients and also helps you learn how to maintain them.

The Purchase Cycle Takes Time

A customer can buy your product a week or even months after coming across your business website. You cannot be sure about it since it relies on the product you are selling and the significance it has for a client. Traffic acquisition channel only interests high-potential clients, but this still does not assure you of any purchase. Use of sales funnels first makes them sign up, and you get their concentration at an initial stage. You comfortably enjoy this privilege when you have your clients' email addresses. Once you have made the potential clients sign up, then you can easily give them regular updates of the products, provide them with the worth of the products, and also issue more information about the products you are selling. You can do this until you have the clients buying your products. After that, they naturally buy your products without you using much effort to convince them. Having an instant purchase cycle for your online business shows why ClickFunnels are vital.

Building More Trust

Unlike in the past where clients only bought from enterprises, there is trust in the use of sales funnel. You can create loyalty with your clients because the opportunity is highly available. This is possible because with ClickFunnels, for example, you can always send automatic emails to newly-registered people informing them about what products you are offering and their value too. It gives you a chance to advertise your products, and create an awareness to them on their policies and procedures. This is what I have personally used sales funnels for, and whenever I give them a product worth, they quickly become loyal. This is another reason why you should incorporate ClickFunnels.

Email Subscribers Do Convert

The pillar in digital sales funnel is emailing. Emails are figuratively highly more powerful in gaining fresh clients than any their social media platform, generally because of their superwave power in the advertising industry. I, for instance, previously initiated a digital career guide to an email list of around 200 registered members and made approximately 50 sales. That is around a 20% alteration quota which is relatively higher than any advertising channel. This shows that you can comfortably exploit emails' power as a booster in your sales. It also confirms that emails are a pillar in the ClickFunnels. Emails have proven to give good feedback in any digital business; hence, they can help you in your business too. Having your email subscribers convert this highly is a reason why you should incorporate ClickFunnels in your business today.

Sales Funnels Can Increase Forever

Most analog enterprises use the buy-and-done sort of activity, where the clients only buy products and leaves. Evidently, in such a situation, the seller does not have time to form a strong relationship with his or her client; hence, no loyalty is established. This will naturally lead to lack of repetitive business sales. When it comes to sales funnels, a client buying the product is only the start of the journey. In sales funnels, repetitive clients buy many times more than one-stop clients which increases your sales. This means that your online profits will always be made higher by these repetitive clients. You see, this sort of sales cannot occur in one-stop clients. Sales funnels are what you need since you will continuously sell products to your loyal customers for so long. This elaborates why you, as an upcoming enterpriser should seriously invest in ClickFunnels among other platforms, if you want to increase a lifetime value for your products.

In Conclusion

Sales funnels are the pillars in the advertising industry today because for one:

- Sales funnels initiate a sure worth of clients which allows you to sell them your products repetitively.

- They let you initiate a relationship that will be forever with your clients at a very initial stage in the sales funnel.

- Sales funnels give you the ability to send emails to clients to advertise your products or services.

- They help you to create a client's loyalty base and lure them into buying your products. This, then, concludes that a platform like ClickFunnels is one of the best to use for your online sales.

Chapter 4: The Purpose of a Strong Pipeline

One of the hardest things for a salesperson to do when he wants to shift from a peddler to a demand creator is remodeling the relation he has with the pipeline. As a peddler moves up the chain, he comprehends that quality is more vital than quantity. As you progress, that can make the pipeline weaker. Sales is like playing with numbers and marketers have always felt that pipelines have more opportunities due to this.

As a salesperson, I have come to realize that there is no reality in most pipelines.

There are several adverse effects in concentrating on quantity. They include:

- Development of an urgency mindset which makes salespersons not make any decisions on controlling their policies

- Pipeline reports lack importance, and small enterprises lack vital knowledge to analytically assess where they stand and make crucial changes in the required format

- Lack of time for marketers to invest in the

preferred opportunities

- Time wastage due to concentrating on unnecessary chances

Demand creators firmly believe that development begins with a robust picturesque view of reality (Davidoff, 2012). Focussing on quality opportunities is vital since it helps a salesperson on the run from commonality.

Creating the change from a pipeline which has so many names to one with lesser names is not advisable, and it's vital to gain the effortless growth that you as a salesperson always wanted over the years.

Tips on Strong Pipeline Construction

- ***Know your worth:*** Clients want loyalty and outcomes. Ensure you show your potential client that you have some expertise in your field to prevent them from making the wrong decision. It also makes them trust the solution you are giving them.

- ***Offer valuable information:*** Make sure you always make yourself unnoticeable to clients as a salesperson. It will help a potential client make the best decision. Ensure you give your potential client reliable information. Let them know the importance of your solution by first using it.

- **Your prospects are future customers:** Make the customers realize why they need to trade with you. Even though the buyer may not buy anytime soon, they will eventually buy from you since you previously interacted with them.

- **Divide your clients to focus on individual needs:** Set an objective that shows your clients your solution will solve their problem. Clients always want everything to be tailor-made. But note that excessively sending too many messages or emails never guarantees a salesperson any reply. It becomes annoying to the client.

- **Every customer is crucial:** Every potential client should be treated equally since they are all critical. Ignoring a potential client and choosing them over another will you make as a salesperson lose many clients to your competitors.

- **Help customers to be successful:** Worth is developed by assisting potential client's in enterprise challenge. Not only should you sell your solution but also go above and beyond what is expected of you. Make all your clients feel appreciated.

- *Find about the people you would like as customers:* Research on who you would want to be your customers but do not force them to be. Instead, leave them to fit your client profile and use your experience to you acquire a firm growth of the business. Then, let fate lead your efforts.

- *Show leadership skills:* Develop leadership views which fascinate potential clients. Make yourself known to potential clients. That will make them buy from you comfortably since they will be ready to trust in your brand.

- *Identifying your prospects never stops:* Do not let a sale come before a potential client. Always let your client come before anything else to succeed as a salesperson. The objective is developing a steady relationship with potential clients, which will make them believe in the solution you have to offer them.

- *Implement ways to engage your prospects:* Cultivation enables you to develop a relationship with potential clients. Even though a client will have set his or her mind on what to buy, as a salesperson, involve your client in indirect sales association by giving them data that can benefit them.

A Strong Pipeline Needs Email Marketing

First of all, emails are very cheap to use, and you can use them to communicate with people.

Everyone today has to go through their emails several times a day. So, there are chances of them stumbling upon your emails which ensures that they get the message you send.

You can customize your emails as much as you want to make the client feel like you are directly talking to him.

Making it a direct email makes your clients feel special since the email is tailored for them.

Email Marketing Needs an Email List

If you start emailing recklessly, then you will not have any good outcomes. It will be a waste of time.

Ensure that before emailing, you have unique designs and a well-organized list. This can be done by ensuring a few things, some of which are listed below:

- Quality. Every salesperson wishes to have people who check their emails regularly and so should you.

- Volume. In this case, which comes right after you highly concentrate on the quantity.

- Relevance. Give information that entails your design and company.

We will see all about email lists later in the book.

Chapter 5: Know Your Target Audience and Qualify Your Prospects

In today's economic world, having a well-defined target audience is all that is required to have a successful business. This calls for you as an entrepreneur to have a sales funnel for your business. It works by reducing the number of prospects to those that have the potential of buying from you. That is the market that you are concerned about.

You might think that you must need a well-publicized popular system to create a sales funnel for your business. That is not true. ClickFunnels is a software that might be of help to you. It is an online sales-funnel builder that will help you build your sales funnel much quicker. With ClickFunnels, there are already pre-built sales funnels, and all you have to do is choose the one that matches with your business.

Once you have selected the appropriate sales funnel, the next step is to build it. You create it by first identifying the target market. It involves the parties that can be interested in your product or services. The goal here is to drive the interested parties into the wide end of your funnel. Later, you will then be able to qualify the prospects and major on the most important. This is the ultimate goal of a sales funnel.

So how do you choose your target audience? Here are some tips that can be of help to you.

Identifying and Analyzing Your Target Market

Finding about your target audience means doing the needed research in your niche. Here are some questions that will help you with that:

- How can you describe your business, or what you are offering?

- How will your customer benefit from your business or offers?

- How do your potential prospects shop?

After now identifying the niche market, you can now go ahead and do some target market analysis. The target market analysis will help in attracting prospects. Here are some pointers that might help in the review:

Gather Intel

Before settling down for a particular audience, you

have to gather some information about the audience. How is the target market going to affect your business? Is it worth it?

Here are some questions that you will have to ask yourself.

- How large is your potential customer base in relation to what you are offering?

- What do you need to change in your proposal for the audience out there to hear you?

- How can you offer your products or services in a way that will maximize the profit potential?

- How can you optimize your marketing efforts to persuade the promising buyers?

Create Customer Profiles and Market Segments

Once you have determined the impact of your target audience on your business, it is now time to get to know your audience.

In most cases, the customers that want your product, usually share a similar trait. By crafting a customer's profile, you can be able to uncover this unique behavior or characteristic (Ferenzi, 2019).

To craft the profile, you can start with the demographic aspect of your customers. This might involve their location, age, gender, income level, and also maybe the education level. After this has been determined, you can now delve into the psychological aspect. It will help you to paint a clearer picture of who your customer is. The mental element may include interests, hobbies, attitudes, and also their behaviors.

You might also include some more attributes that you think can go deeper in knowing your audience more. Be creative. Remember that the better you know your customer, the better you can sell to them.

Once all this has been done, you can be assured of a high starting point in seizing a target market.

Be Specific

Most businesses usually target audiences like the youth, the working class, or the stay-at-home moms. These are generally not wrong choices at all. You, however, need to specify such choices since they appear to be so general. So, instead of saying that the youth is your target market, talk of the millennials. That is more specific.

As a new entrepreneur, you might have a fear of being too specific. You think that you might limit your reach in the process. In reality, what you are doing is setting yourself up for long-term success. This is because you will now be making informed decisions that are dictated by your loyal customers.

Therefore, yearn to drill down to more specific aspects about your customers so that you can set yourself apart from the competition.

By following these three rules, you will now have identified your prospects. You will then focus on them and attract them to the wide end of the sales funnel. Once this has been done, all that will remain is to identify the most committed customers. This will now become your primary targets for your products.

So, how do you segregate the committed customers from the lot? These two steps might help with that:

1. *Conduct your primary research*

Primary research can go a long way in letting you understand your audience. You will gather data directly from your customers. With this data, you can be able to know which customers are really into your product or services and work on engaging them.

A downside to primary research is that it is expensive. However, you will reap so much from it.

2. *Look at your business in a fresh light*

At this stage, you already know to whom you are selling to. However, due to the shift in the market place, your clientele might change. So, you should always keep data on your target audience up to date. This is by conducting primary research regularly. It will help in refining your product strategy and brand voice.

You will also gain in being one step ahead of your competitors.

Conclusion

In conclusion, in creating a sales funnel, you have to work smart. Using a platform like ClickFunnels will help you build your sales funnel much faster.

The working of a sales funnel is just like how a funnel works. You have to attract a large number of customers and drive them to the wide end of the funnel. Later, you can qualify your customers and choose the most committed ones. This will increase the effectiveness of your advertising strategy.

What are you waiting for!

Chapter 6: Building Your Buyers Persona

As an entrepreneur, you should first know who your buyer is before delving into paid advertising. Knowing your committed customers first will increase your advertising effectiveness.

It is for this reason that ClickFunnels provide a template whereby you can get to understand your core customer groups. This, therefore, calls for you as an entrepreneur to create buyer personas.

Defining the Buyer's Persona

Having a buyer's persona means having a pictured representation of your potential prospects based on what you have found out about them i.e. using research from the wide market and data from your current customers.

For you to create your buyer persona, you have to look at some critical pointers from your customers. These pointers include customer demographics, behavior patterns, motivations, and goals. You should not, however, shy away from adding a few other pointers to this list. The more detailed you are, the better.

When creating a buyer persona, you should be very specific. Buyer personas provide tremendous insight and structure for your company. They are going to determine where you will focus your time and also guide your product development.

Why Are Buyer Personas Important?

In today's world, online space is becoming more and more crowded. The improvement of technology mainly causes this. It is, therefore, easy for anyone to create campaigns that target customers. It is for this reason that you as an entrepreneur should yearn to have some ultra-targeted advertisements for your business. This will help you set yourself apart from the crowd.

In the past, ultra-targeted Ads and communications were only used by large companies. It was costly. However, times have changed immensely. Nowadays, even you as a small online retailer can have access to a particular audience targeting with just a tiny budget (Lazazzera, n.d.).

A platform like ClickFunnels provides you with easy access to your specific audience at a minimal fee that encompasses more features. With this platform, you can advance your targeting based on aspects like the location, age, language spoke, education level, and also the interests. This will, therefore, go a long way in reducing the burden associated with finding the right target market.

Personas Will Evolve and Change

With the changing economic environment, personas are deemed to change. As you learn more about your committed customers, you will have different ideas about your buyer personas. You will now be able to determine what motivates your real customers. This will, therefore, call for you to take a step back and redefine your persona again so that you can target your potential customers effectively.

How to Create Buyer Personas

Buyer personas are usually just like a refined version of your target customers. Therefore, for you to create a buyer persona, you have to do some research on your target market. This research will help you get to know the needs and interests of your market. This research can be done by carrying out surveys or even interviewing your target audience.

With a platform like ClickFunnels, knowing your buyer personas can be easy. Why is this?

- ClickFunnels provides a platform where you can reach an extensive customer database. You can, therefore, learn about how consumers consume your content.

- ClickFunnels has already pre-built templates for your sales funnel where consumers get to fill in their personal information in those form fields. This will make it easy for you to group personas according to informational leads.

- ClickFunnels provides pre-built templates which you can use to converse with your customers. Here, you can interview them and get to know what they like about your product.

The last point is the most vital and I will be discussing it in detail below.

Finding Interviewees to Help You Research Your Buyer Persona

Having people to talk to as you research your buyer

persona is one of the most vital steps. This means that you will have to carry out some interviews to get to know what motivates your audience.

The question that remains now is who exactly do you interview? How do you find your interviewees? There are a few sources you should tap into. They include:

Customers

Your customer is the perfect place for you to start interviewing. They have already purchased your product or engaged with your company in one way or the other.

The thing to note here is that in choosing the customers to interview, do not focus more on the 'good' customers. These are the customers that are going to praise you all day long. As good as that feels, it is not healthy for your business. You should try and engage the 'bad' customers too. These are the customers that are going to criticize your business and products. By doing this, you will have a greater insight into the persona that you want.

An advantage of interviewing customers is that you will not need to give them an incentive — customers like being heard. So, when you open up to their world and the challenges they face, you will be doing them an excellent service. Interviewing customers will also make them feel involved in the business. This will cause them to be very loyal to your company.

It will be a win-win situation.

Prospects

To balance your interview, you should also interview people that have not yet bought your product. These people are your prospects.

Referrals

Now in a case whereby you are venturing in a new market, you do not have customers. You might also not have prospects. In such cases, you need some referrals to talk to people who may fit into your target personas. You might reach out to your circle of friends or even social media contacts to help you find people you would like to get introduced to and interview.

This process, however, may take a longer time and may be tough to get a large volume of people. Nonetheless, you can reap some very high-quality interviews out of it.

Tips for Recruiting Interviewees

To find potential interviewees, you must first have a pool of people that are willing to be interviewed. Here are ways that you can attract many willing interviewees:

Use Incentives

People who have no relationship with your business can be hard to lure them into interviews. By use of an incentive, they will now have a reason to participate. You can provide an incentive like a gift card for every interviewee.

This, however, does not apply everywhere. Some customers are willing to participate without an incentive.

Be Clear This Is Not a Sales Call

This is usually important to the non-customers. You must assure them that you are just doing research and that you are after the challenges they face in their lives.

Make It Easy To Say Yes

Make the customer feel as if they are of value in the interview. It will make them feel the urge to participate in the conversation. This is by, maybe, letting them set the time at which they are willing to be interviewed.

Twenty Questions to Ask In Persona Interviews

Once you have now identified your interviewees, it is now time to ask some questions! This is obviously after the greetings and usual small talk.

To create a whole persona's profile, there are different categories of questions that you need to ask. Here are some of the groups and the issues you should ask about in each group.

Role

1. What tasks do you perform in your job? Who are you in your job?

2. How do you measure your role at work?

3. How can you describe your daily schedule?

4. Which skills do you need to perfect your work?

5. Do you use any tools or knowledge in your job?

6. Do you answer to anyone? Who is responsible of answering to you?

Organization

7. Which industry matches with your business role?

8. How large or small is your company or business?

Goals

9. Do you know what you are supposed to do?

10. What effects does success bring in your role?

Problems

11. Which problems do you find hard to tackle?

Collecting Useful Information

12. How does new information about your job reach you?

13. Do you read any blogs or published content?

14. Do you participate in any groups or social media gatherings?

Personal Background

15. Describe your demographics.

16. Describe your educational background.

17. Describe your career path.

Shopping Approach

18. What's your way of interacting with sellers?

19. Do you research about the sellers or products on the internet?

20. Describe how you purchased your latest product or service.

Identifying the Number of People to Interview

It's unfortunate that there is no specific number to the interviews you can have. It all depends on how much you have known your persona. Three to five meetings for each category of interviewees can, however, be a good starting point.

You can also apply the rule of thumb. Are you accurately predicting what the interviewee is likely to say? Then it's time to stop. Why? It shows you have already grasped the patterns of your interviewees.

How to Use Your Research to Create Your Persona

At this point, you have completed the interviews, and you have some raw data from your potential and current customers. So, what do you do with this information? How do you distill all of that data, so it is easily digestible to your team?

The next step, therefore, is to take all that data and identify patterns and similarities from the answers you got from the interviews. Using these patterns, you can create at least one primary persona and share that persona with the rest of the company.

Fill in Your Persona's Necessary Demographic Information

At this stage, fill all the demographic information about your persona. If you didn't feel comfortable asking about this in the interview, you could carry out an online survey. Most people are more comfortable disclosing things like this through a study rather than verbal communication.

Discuss With Your Team about What Motivates Your Persona

At this stage, distill all the information you got after asking the 'Why' questions.

Get Your Team Prepared For Knowing the Persona

You now make your sales team conversant with who the persona is and what they need. You can also go a step further and create some challenges that your organization may face and try to solve them. This will make them feel prepared to address the issues during conversations with the consumers.

Help Crafting Messaging For Your Persona

Tell people how to talk about your product. This will ensure everyone in the company is speaking the same language when having conversations with consumers.

Conclusion

Finally, make sure you give your persona name. You can also include a real-life image to your persona. This will make your team truly envision what the persona looks like.

With this done, you now know the kind of person you are attracting using your sales funnel.

Chapter 7: The Lead Magnet

If you are a website owner looking forward to more customer conversions, at times, the following scenario happens as time progresses:

You work very hard by waking up early to write content for your blog or maybe spend money to get it done. As you write, there are relevant titles that you need to address, and you have all of them lined up. You find the relevant keywords to match the titles and what customers are looking before composing everything to meaningful articles. After about a month or two, traffic grows to a considerable number, say, 10,000 followers.

By the time you are reaching such a number, you are suffering from exhaustion, and the number of followers is just followers. Your bank is not reflecting your efforts. After about six months, the number of followers is either still the same or slightly lower.

If that is the case for you, then it is clear that you, me, and everyone else going through the same that there is something missing.

After years of searching, I finally found something valuable that can solve the more customers' problem and also increase the conversion rate.

I need a landing page that can collect customer

information so that I can focus on the individuals later. How do I do that? By using a lead magnet.

Lead Magnet Definition

Some people will call it the gated content. It is simply that popup or space on your landing page that offers something that a customer can use – a free demo, pdf download, something to try out, etc.

The reason why marketers use this tactic is so that as the customers reach out for the information, you are getting something in return, mostly, their email address. Having a lead magnet on the website is a massive marketing tool that brands have been using to generate business leads.

There are numerous examples that you can use all through your marketing funnel, but the key thing here is to use content that matches the buyer's journey to acquiring your product (Mialki, 2018). What I mean here is that you cannot, for example, offer a product to a customer who doesn't know what you are doing.

Anyway, the end result of a lead magnet is to generate an email list, get some loyal customers, generate meaningful leads, then convert the leads into buying options for customers.

Lead Magnet Purpose

A lead magnet can do two things for you. The first one is to collect information from potential customers – the prospects. People are always worried about issuing their contacts, but if they get something back, they will do it. Most customers who don't get what they are looking for never come back. Since you don't want to be one of the unfortunate online sellers, a lead magnet can help you from customers skipping your offers.

The second thing that a lead magnet can do is to get to know your customer. That happens if you a well-constructed sales funnel like in ClickFunnels. A high percentage of customers can never buy from you're the first time they land on your site. A lead magnet should be there to lead to take consideration. This way, you will be warming things up as they get ready to buy.

With that, what can your audience use as a lead magnet?

Creating a Lead Magnet?

You have probably visited a website that requested you to feel in some information for a free guide download on an issue you just read content about on the same website. That popup or small space with input tabs on the page is what we are talking about. So, this is not about writing some lengthy content to grab user contacts.

Consider it as something like 'Tips to make the best lead magnets for your online business' with a downloading button below where the user is supposed to fill in their email address.

For you to generate more leads, your lead magnet should be:

- Easy to understand

- Offering something valuable that prospects are likely to go for when you ask them to.

With that, here is the checklist to follow as you consider creating your lead magnet.

Who Is Your Target Customer?

Before you do anything, first identify the customers you want to attract. Your magnet requires absolute relevance to the specific needs of your target customers. If you don't address their wants, they will not trust what you offer, and that will exclude them from considering and buying.

What Is Your Value Proposition?

Have you gotten your targets? Now, it's time to give them the reason why they should take your offer. That means the value of subscribing to your emails or whatever you are selling. At times, that might drive marketers to get a product that they think will be useful to customers, but that is not really the way to go. Think or look for a problem that your prospects are facing and use that to reach out by providing a solution. That is what will get you to a selling point.

Choosing a Format

You can design and offer a lead magnet as you please but remember that there is a marketing funnel to follow and the customer has a journey to make. In the different stages, here is what you can consider:

The Awareness Stage

At this juncture, prospects are looking for solutions to problems, but they don't know what to pick or leave. Use that as a way to educate them about your brand and raising general awareness. Realizing conversions here should take into account a form where the potential buyers can fill some information about themselves. Do not include too many inputs for filling. A name and email address are enough.

Some of the things that you can include in your lead magnet include:

- Reports

- Subscription to blogs

- Tips

- eBooks

Consideration Stage

After your prospects find a solution from you, they begin to compare you with similar brands that offer the same. At that point, your lead magnet can attempt to acquire more information from the customers than what you required in the awareness stage. Some of the things that can lead to more contact information include:

- White papers

- Videos

- Case studies

- Podcasts

- Webinars

- Free samples

The Decision Stage

Reaching this point is what marketers are always looking for. It means that those who have joined you have known you, compared with you with other problem solvers and they now want to purchase what you are offering. The lead magnet at this point should show off something that will make the prospects request for more information from you.

What you can offer includes:

- Discounts

- Free trials

- Consultations

- Demos

Creating Content for the Lead Magnet

Once you have known what to offer, it is time to write what you are going to offer them. As you write, here are some of the tips to use as a guideline as you create something meaningful to the readers.

- ***Specify:*** Focus on giving a solution to a problem. Write something precise that answers questions as it solves what the prospects are looking for. That makes it easy for people to read and understand what you are offering.

- **Be unique:** Offering something that can't be ignored means writing original content. If the users can find it by just searching on Google or Bing, then you are not worth giving that in your lead magnet.

- **Efficiency:** If you have already worked on some emails or posts, you can tune them to fit the context of your lead if you want to be fast in giving out a solution. The point here is to make sure that your content matches what you are offering at each stage.

- **Establish authority:** For the prospects to trust what you are offering them, you must be dependable. That means demonstrating your expertise in the field with certainty. The prospects need to see that you can actually do it. As you write, avoid phrases like 'I think' since they show that you are not certain.

Promoting Your Lead Magnet

At this point, most of the work is done. It's now all about your customers finding your target. The next question is, how do you expose the target to your prospects? Here are some of the promoting tips.

On Your Website

You can look at your web pages to know which page will serve as the smartest option. Consider the following:

- **Homepage:** Put it as a popup, on the sidebar, or the footer.

- **Blog index page:** You can put there in posts that relate to what you are offering.

- **Resource page:** You can also use it where you have all your resources centralized. The dedicated page will carry all your white papers or subscriptions for example and having a lead magnet there can be useful.

- **Thank you page:** In the page where you are thanking people, you can offer them something else using a lead magnet.

- **Error page:** When visitors see the 404 message, you can use a lead magnet to redirect them to your offers.

On Social Media

Consider the following features:

- Updating your status with an image linking to your website. Aim at the landing page.

- Participate in social media groups by entering discussion topics and include the relevant links in there.

- Create ads for the available social media platforms. Ads for Facebook, Instagram, Twitter, and the rest.

Content Hubs

There are various platforms that offer advertising venues since people already go there to seek information. With that, you can check the following out:

- A forum that can allow you to ask or post or answer a question such as Medium Daily.

- Q&A websites where people ask and answer questions such as Yahoo! Answers or Quora Digest.

- Aggregator sites where you can post some news

which can be ranked using a voting system such as Reddit.

Where Else Can You Use A Lead Magnet?

If you know a place that content can be consumed, you can get creative, and make your magnet get people there.

- Paid adverts such as banners, native ads, PPC ads

- Putting the lead magnet at the end of a webinar as a way for the attendees to get more information.

- If you don't have a podcast to talk about your offers, look for someone who can feature you in theirs.

- You can partner with companies that offer newsletters and request to be featured there. You can link the feature to your lead magnet or the landing page.

It's Time to Do It

Regardless of how you want to advertise, the aim here is to lead the prospects to your magnet. If you want to grow your email list and contact information, lead magnets are a great way to help you do so. I have done that with ClickFunnels and also advertised on different platforms already, and the list is growing to numbers I didn't imagine before I started.

Remember to promote your magnet with a good landing page that can increase conversions.

Chapter 8: Creating a Great Landing Page

If you can't get a good web designer to work on your landing page, there are ready templates like in ClickFunnels to help you do that. So, creating one is not one of those complex subjects that you are thinking about.

On the other hand, it involves more than creating something 'good looking' since giving your prospects what they want will need a lot of research. So, we are not going to focus on how to create a great landing page, but we are going to look at some of the things that an outstanding landing page should consider.

There is no one guide for all who need to create a landing page since different marketers will want different things for their potential customers. Let's look at the following instances:

- Your friend needs a landing page that will help him sell the running outfit to athletes.

- You want a landing page to invite people to your webinar about how to generate online sales.

- Another person out there needs a landing page for people to take an online quiz.

Do you think the three scenarios can follow the same guide to achieve results? Every marketer here needs a different audience, products, industry, focus, cost, messaging options, and testimonials just to mention a few.

Since it is clear that no one size will fit all, we will check on a few fundamentals pertaining to creating a landing page that works for your marketing niche. By the end of this chapter, you will have all the points you need to create your landing page without further research apart from what you need for the prospects.

What Is A Landing Page?

First, let us see what a landing page is and how it differs from the rest of your pages on your website. A landing page is that page on your site that is responsible for raising the conversion rates as you strive to reach your business goals (Patel, 2018). It could be your homepage or another page on the website or a specific page that serves as your campaign area for what you are offering.

When we talk about a landing page, it is different from the rest of the pages on your site in that it has different access. If you look at a homepage, for example, people can know about it by telling them or sharing a link on social media among other means. For landing pages, you need keywords and search results ranking on the first page. Such a page will need promotion or ad words or something similar since it exists to do one thing only: convert customers to buyers.

Your homepage can serve as a landing page if you set it to increase the conversions.

Advantages of an Effective Landing Page

Here are some of the benefits bound to come your way if you have something that is indeed attracting the customers.

Increase Your SEO Ranking

Google is using SEO to rank search results which means your landing page should already have some target keywords that match what the customers look for while on the internet. Marketers go further to use Google Adwords and other paid boosts. All of these make the landing page to move up and get your product within customer's vicinity.

Promoting Something Gaining the Awareness

A landing page has something in specific to promote or sell out. It is not the same as what other pages on the site and it is there to give out one message all across the customer base. That means you can focus on one of the marketing goals and move it to the forefront to get more conversions. It also gives you the opportunity to track how one of your products is performing in the market.

Help Customers Get Into Your Funnel

If your landing page is converting sales as expected, it acts as a portal where customers can join you or get what you are offering faster. Instead of people looking for ways to join your offers by navigating your site, the landing page makes that easier.

Considerations before Making a Landing Page

- ***Your end goal:*** When visitors get to your page, what do you want them to do? Whatever your objective is, determine what you need them to do so that you can track the conversions later in the same manner as you designed.

- ***Your substitutes:*** You need to check on who else is offering the same products or services as you, how they are doing it, and how you can follow suit. If your competitors have something that is helping people out there, you better do the same.

- ***Your prospects:*** Who are you targeting? What do they need and what do they aspire for? It may sound obvious, but it will get you what they need. If you understand what the customer needs, then it will be easier to cater to their needs. If you don't, then it will be hard to design a persuasive copy that follows the customer requirements.

- ***How the customers get to your landing page:*** You can design your message in such a way that users from different platforms can get it as they read from where they first saw your advertisement. Businesses with more landing pages target different platforms such as Google, Facebook, and Twitter which leads to more conversions than those who have just one landing page. It is, however, hard to get more landing pages so if you are starting up, start with a custom one, then add as you continue to get more masses from other platforms.

How to Make Great Landing Pages

After going through the landing page overview, here are some persuasive points that will help you make an outstanding page.

- **Short, sweet, and precise:** A proper landing page should carry the necessary information about what you are offering that is just enough. Nothing too much to overwhelm the reader or visitor which will make them click away.

- **Content that inspires confidence:** As the information lures the visitor in, what you say should be rich in authority as you stick to relevance.

- **All roads head to the endpoint:** The links on your landing page should lead visitors to your offer. That means eliminating anything that will lead them away such as links serving as exit points. If they should leave the funnel, the link used should not be as evident as the one requiring them to get in.

- **Easy conversions:** Another objective on your landing page is to make it easy for visitors to convert. The prompt to join should be followed by something easier to comprehend which implies getting rid of barriers that will make them think otherwise. If people are supposed to submit forms, make it irresistible. If you want them to download something, make a button that they cannot let go.

- **Smooth design:** You should have a clear design that answers all the questions with easy navigation where necessary. Avoid having pop-ups in the middle unless you need to. The simplest way for customers to convert is to make sure that conversion is only a click away.

- **Precise CTA:** A call to action should be somewhere on the headline title or on the button to be clicked. It should be something that tells the visitor what to do. Something like 'Get started' or 'Submit Your Copy Now' will increase conversions since it's telling users to act.

- **Catchy headlines:** In most cases, the landing page will have the headline introducing the offer and the subheading explaining more about the value proposition. To hit the nail on the head, you can use the heading as a line that introduces the visitor and gives them the value at the same time.

- **Engaging content:** Use words that will make the visitor feel engaged. Using the words 'you' when referring to the reader makes them feel connected. A word like 'imagine' will make them visualize about your offers.

- ***It's about the visitor:*** Don't start telling the visitor about yourself and what you do. They can read that in the about section on our website. Go straight to what you are providing and how it can help them achieve the solution they are looking for.

- ***Use a video when necessary:*** Videos offer a better way to educate visitors if your product is complex as they get entertained.

- ***Easy scanning at a glance:*** Visitors on your page have a short time to get what you are offering, join, or go away. Consider the time as eight seconds. Make your page easy to scan by highlighting the main points and using bullets if you have more information. Coloring your information hierarchy also works here.

- ***Appropriate and excellent imagery:*** Visitors like to look at bright pictures that relate to what you are offering on your landing page. Consider having some good pictures and using something that directs users on what to do such as arrows showing the route to follow.

- ***Match your landing page with the correct ad***

text: For a landing page to work as expected, you need to match your keywords with what is in the PPC ad text. That will assure that your visitors are following the same path. Don't use words that will lead them elsewhere or lead to somewhere they can get the product or service you are offering.

- *Only ask what visitors can give:* If you have more fields to fill in before they get to your product, then you are decreasing your chances of scooping more customers. If you need more information, then you can do that later on the thank you page after they have acquired something from you.

- *Use color to lure:* The color on your button should be something brighter than what is on the background. Most buttons are red, orange, or green since the colors are a better way to give contrast and increase visibility.

- *Consider being mobile friendly:* Since a visitor could be using any smart device to view your landing page, make sure the view incorporates the small screens by using the necessary adjustments as you construct the landing page.

With the points above plus an overview of a landing page, it is now clear that you need one if you want to increase your conversion rate. Those who have been using landing pages ahead of you have realized a lot of benefits and customers. ClickFunnels is one of the platforms that you can use for great landing pages ideas and much more to guide you on making more conversions from what you create.

Chapter 9: Giving an Upset Offer on the Back End

As an entrepreneur, having some loyal customers is a thing that assures you of success in your venture. For you to have these loyal customers, you must first generate some leads. A sales funnel serves as your blueprint for nurturing these leads. After nurturing these leads, you must work to keep these leads.

As simple as the concept sounds, building a sales funnel that will convert prospects to committed customers can be very challenging. You will be forced to create landing pages and offers for opportunities at every stage in the buying journey.

However, with a platform like ClickFunnels, all this work can be reduced to just a few clicks. ClickFunnels will help you in converting and retaining customers. How? By allowing you to create funnels that will promote the customer service of your venture.

What Is Customer Service?

Customer service is the role dedicated to helping

customers get the value they paid for from a product or service, especially when things go wrong. Customers are usually the most critical aspect of your business. The service you offer them must be outstanding. Customer service though is traditionally undervalued due to its reliance on so-called soft skills. This is, however, an old point of view. Nowadays, customer support is more of technical ability than natural talent (Ciotti, 2019). More and more enterprises are becoming more creative in ways that they can improve their customer service.

This, therefore, calls for you as an entrepreneur to become great at the distinct and ever-evolving skill set needed for customer service. Skills for customer service are usually tailored according to the business. However, some essential skills can lay the groundwork for all the rest.

Skills to Improve Your Customer Service

Know Your Product Inside Out

There is nothing as bad for a customer, like asking a question about a product to get wrong or incomplete answer about it. This provokes the customer's liking of your product. It does not matter how good your product is. It is like a singer forgetting the lyrics of their song onstage.

It is, therefore, essential for you and your staff to know the product you are selling in-depth. Know what your product is, what it entails, and also maybe how it is used. This will go a long way in reducing the awkward moments and increase your customer satisfaction.

You can also go a step further and train new hires on what your product is and how it benefits the consumers even if they are just part-time employees.

You cannot provide excellent customer service without being an expert on your product.

Learn To Use Positive Language

The use of positive communication, more often than not, yields a positive reaction from the customers. By a positive language, it does not mean that you should confine yourself to artificial cheery and upbeat tone. No, it is more of avoiding the negative phrasing during communications with the customers.

Customers hate being lectured on what you cannot do for them. They want you to provide an alternative to how they can solve the problem at hand. Show them that you are committed to finding a solution to the problem. This will go a long way in keeping your customers close.

Here is a negative and positive way to approach a particular problem:

NEGATIVE: "It appears as if that product won't be available for a few weeks, so I can't place an order for you until it arrives at our warehouse."

POSITIVE: "It looks like that product will be available next month. I can place an order for you as soon as it reaches our warehouse."

Adapt To Your Tone to the Context

For every business communication, there are two fundamental aspects that you as an entrepreneur should put into consideration. This is the voice and the tone that you use. The voice is the underlying style that you want your brand to have. The tone, on the other hand, is the appropriate style for a specific context.

Take for example an enterprise that sells beverages. For such a company, they can promote their brand by maybe supporting fun through every drink that the customers buy. In such a case, the voice of the company will all surround the fact they are fun. However, in instances where a customer gets a late shipment of their product, that voice needs to change. This is now where the tone comes into play. You should match the tone with the conversational style of your customer but still maintain the voice of your brand.

Therefore, stay consistent, and use your brand voice as a foundation while adjusting your tone based on the customer's temperament and their reason for contacting you.

Crystal-Clear Writing Skills

For you to improve on your customer service, miscommunication is an element that you would try to avoid at all costs. Miscommunication, more often than not, is usually brought about by unclear messaging. Most enterprises major on clever writing at the expense of clear writing. This does not mean that being creative is wrong. Creativity is an integral part of making your messages stand out. However, creativity should not be a priority. You must first yearn to make your messaging as clear as possible to the consumer.

Clear messaging can be achieved through the use of simple to understand words. You should also avoid making assumptions about what customers know. It is not everyone that knows what you know.

For example, if you want a customer to share their address, in cases when you are delivering a product to them, don't just tell them to send you an address. Provide step-by-step directions that your customer can follow until that is achieved.

Another thing to consider is the way you style your replies, especially over email. You should use features like bullets, line breaks, and also boldfaces to favor easy reading. This will avoid confusion because your message will now be in easily scannable sections.

Advocacy for Your Customers

Typically, businesses are expected to have empathy for their customers. Understanding, however, is not enough for your customers. More critical than empathy is advocacy.

Advocacy is championing the concerns of your customers and being active in identifying potential solutions. It usually works because unlike empathy, it is more of an active act than a passive one. The consumer, in this case, can feel your action and thus can identify your presence.

For advocacy to work, you have to understand the phases of customer interactions which are:

- *Sensing:* This is when you try and figure out what caused the customer's issue. It should happen at the start of the conversation.

- **Seeking:** After now pinpointing the problem, you can now explore all the possible solutions at your disposal.

- **Settling:** Once all the solutions have now surfaced, you can now talk with your consumer on the best solution to settle on. This solution should bring out the best outcome.

Advocacy now comes in during the "seeking" phase. By telling the customer about the solutions you have explored, they can even become more receptive to a less than perfect outcome. However, you should explain the answer in a way that the consumer will see the logic that led you to suggest what you did. This will make them more understanding.

If you provide a weak solution to the consumer, he or she will have the picture that you are just trying to brush them off. The last thing that you would want for your business is to appear as if you are uncaring. This will damage your customer service.

So, yearn to take control of situations and show the customer that you are willing to provide a reliable solution to the problem at hand.

Creativity to Deliver Frugal Wows

What are frugal wows? Frugal wows are gestures that

have no monetary value for a customer but create lasting loyalty through the gesture's thoughtfulness. They usually rely on creativity rather than capital. This means that any entrepreneur can take advantage of the frugal wows to improve on their customer service.

Some of the frugal wows could be like:

- Sending handwritten thank-you notes

- Including creative packaging inserts

- Providing samples that complement a purchase

- Offering surprise post-purchase discounts

- Creating personal connections with short videos

As you grow your business, it is good to find ways to deliver repeatable wow moments. It would also be wise for you to delight many customers a little than one customer a lot.

Therefore, consider the wow moments as a little unexpected extra for your customers, and this will go a long way in helping build your reputation.

Understand How to Set the Right Expectations

When creating a funnel for your customers to interact with, setting the right expectations is very important.

Setting the right expectations can directly influence how the customers perceive the quality of your support.

For example, when setting up your chat widget, you can add detail like "Get an answer instantly". This might look so minor but can cause dissatisfaction of your customers if your average response time is about five minutes. This is a mistake that you could have avoided if only you set the right expectations.

The secret to this is to under-promise and over-deliver. Easy as it sounds, it can be so challenging. There will be times that you will feel the need to over promise to attract more customers. This will increase your internal pressure for you to meet those promises and this is not healthy for the business.

Therefore, be careful with regard to time. Do not make promises in areas that you are sure you have no control over.

Offering A Downsize Option

As an entrepreneur, you have to be aware that budget constraints are a factor that can make you lose your customers. When your customers are having a financial problem, they can, at times, lack the economic power to purchase your product. This can make you lose them.

So, what do you do in such cases to still keep them close? You can create a funnel that will be able to accommodate such kind of customers. Be considerate, and offer cheaper options for such individuals. This will help you in keeping them close.

Keep in mind that those constraints may change. Therefore, leaving them during such times can make you lose them forever.

Conclusion

Finally, through ClickFunnels, you can easily and quickly create a sales funnel that will be able to convert and retain customers. Retaining customers is usually all about how you interact with them. How much support do you provide for them?

The customer service of your business should be at its best for you to retain customers. Involve yourself with the customers and try to be more active. This is by maybe providing solutions to the problems they are facing. It will go a long way in building your reputation.

Chapter 10: Split Testing

The goal of marketing is usually to increase the returns of your venture. However, there are times that your marketing strategy may fail.

So, how do you know that your marketing campaigns are working? Split testing can help you with this. Split testing helps you to know if your marketing efforts are achieving results also shows you where you can make changes to make it more effective.

So what does split testing really mean?

Split Test Definition

It's a method used to test multiple or a single element of a website against each other to see which works best.

If you are new to split testing, you might find all this very complex. Here are some definitions that can make it easier for you to understand.

During split testing, you are just comparing a control version of the website and a variant version. A control version is an original version of whatever you are testing. On the other hand, a variant version is the changed version of your control. The variant is meant to test against the control so as to determine which performs better.

What do we mean by performing better? Split testing is usually a very important part in conversion optimization. A conversion is any action that you want someone to complete, for example, like buying a product. This means that split testing helps in increasing the rate at which people complete the desired task. Therefore, during comparing the control and variant versions, you have to choose the version that aids in quick completion of the task.

In addition, a common name for a split test is usually an A/B test. However, with an A/B test, you divide your web traffic in two, with 50% of your traffic seeing the control and 50% seeing the variant.

Who Split Testing Is Right For

Split testing is usually essential for small businesses that rely on online marketing campaigns as their only way to drive their sales.

Some other types of businesses split testing is right for are like:

- Virtual Business Coaching Businesses

- E-commerce Businesses

- Digital Marketing Companies

- Software Companies

Why Should You Run a Split Test?

A split test can really go a long way in helping you increase the effectiveness of your marketing strategy. Once you suspect that your marketing strategy is failing, you should carry out a split test. You can also carry out a split test in cases where you think that you can get better results through marketing than you are already getting.

Here are some other potential benefits of carrying out a split test:

- Removing guesswork from your marketing approach and increase certainty

- Getting to know how potential customers respond to your offers instead of thinking how they will respond using the data from your survey

- Benefiting from unseen insights that will improve your business

- Creating content that the customers need

Preparing For Your First Split Test

Before you start your first split test, you must first know what you can test. Some of the things you can test are like headlines, page copy, button text, colors, forms, images, and maybe the social sharing buttons. In short, you can test anything that appears on the web page.

To ensure that your split test is effective, here is a tried procedure that you should follow:

Step 1: Observe and Collect Data

This is the most important step. In this step, you will have to observe what's happening on your site or the element that you want to test. Later, you can collect data about it.

Some of the places that you can collect your data are like your web analytics account, where you'll pay attention to top landing pages, entrances and exits, bounces, and if you have set up goals, conversions.

Step 2: Form a Hypothesis

After obtaining the data, you now need a hypothesis. It simply means to have an idea about why you are receiving the results the way they are and how you can work on them to your advantage.

Here is a way that you could form your hypothesis:

- *Analyzed problem:* People clicking on the submit button in your sign up form are not enough. One of the problems could be the button not standing out.

- *Proposed solution:* You believe that by lightening the background, the button can stand out leading to more sign-ups.

- *Success metrics:* You will know that this works when you get an increase of sign-ups by around 10% in the next two weeks.

Step 3: Perform Your Test and Check on Results

In this stage, you will have to use the data you collected in the first step. This data will be used now to measure the results. This will help you know which one between the control and the variant is more effective.

Using ClickFunnels for Split Testing

ClickFunnels is a platform that I usually use for most of my split tests. This is because it already has an in-built A/B split testing functionality. This reduces all the hustle of creating the variant version. When I need to build a check-out page, I usually create a variation with just one click.

Once the split test is set up, ClickFunnels evenly distributes around half of the traffic to the control and the other half to the variation. In addition to this, ClickFunnels also tracks the conversion rate. This, therefore, means that your only work now is to check which version converts better, the control or the variant.

Once you have got sufficient traffic, you can now pick a winner, and the other page gets automatically deleted.

This really reduces the workload and is much quicker with even better results.

Conclusion

In conclusion, a split test is a very important factor for your business. It helps you as an entrepreneur to determine whether or not your marketing strategy is working. This is important because you will avoid the chances of making any losses in your business. A split test can also help you check on the areas that you can improve on your marketing strategy. This will help in increasing the effectiveness of your marketing plan and thus lead to increased sales.

Split testing, however, can be a bit tedious, but with a platform like ClickFunnels, all the hustle can be reduced to just a few clicks. So, join the bandwagon now!

Chapter 11: Call to Actions

When building a sales funnel, an important aspect to consider is the conversion optimization. This is all about how fast your buyers are going to complete a given task like purchasing your product online. However, for the buyers to take that action, you have to provoke a response from them. This is now where the call to action aspect of a sales funnel comes into play.

The call to action aspect is a factor that many people tend to often neglect. Most marketers usually ignore the relevance of the call to action to a sales funnel.

So, what does a call to action really mean?

The Basics of Call to Action

The CTA, as it is normally called, is basically an instruction you give to your audience that provokes an immediate response and gets them to take some sort of action. The action, in this case, can be a lot of things. It really depends on your business. This is because it can be to request them to download an eBook, to purchase a product, or even maybe to register for an event.

The effectiveness of a CTA is usually solely based on

its placement throughout the buyer's journey. You have to be very keen on its placement. Moreover, it is important to use only one call to action rather than use multiple calls to action. This is because it will eliminate the paradox of choice for your buyers.

So, how do you build an effective CTA?

Guide to Building an Effective Call to Action

Brainstorm

Brainstorming is an important first step in creating a call to action. In this step, you must determine the goals of your CTA. This is like maybe asking yourself questions like:

- What kind of action do you want your audience to take?

- What message will best sum up your product?

By answering such questions, you will be able to focus and create better content for your messaging that will get your audience to act.

Start With a Compelling Verb

A compelling verb can be a good way to provoke your audience into action. Remember the goal here is to get your audience to act. A verb can make all the difference for your sales funnel (Parkes, 2018).

So, which kind of verbs should you use? Some of the best compelling verbs can be like download, continue, sign up, subscribe, order, get started, and also find out. You can also do some research and add some other verbs to the list.

Incorporate a Buzzword

Buzzwords can be used to complement the compelling verbs. This will help in really selling your call to action. The thing to note here is that you should be simple when using them. If you carelessly plug multiple buzzwords into your sales funnel, then you might end up losing credibility and trust with your audience.

Some of the buzzwords you might use are like try it for free, get started now, sign up for a free trial and maybe let's do it!

Create Urgency

Remember how it was back in college when you were given some work to do and had to submit it before a certain date. The urgency to complete it before the date forced you into action. This means that deadlines get us to act.

So, by incorporating deadlines to your call to action, you can provide that extra motivator that will get your audience to act. Some of the phrases you can use to create the urgency are like:

- Sign up before the end of the month

- Get it before it's gone

Keep It Simple

Simplicity is a key aspect of your call to action. Your customers are just there to act, not to read a novel. So, the longer the word count of your CTA, the less likely your audience will click on it.

Therefore, if you have a call to action button, the shorter the wording, the better.

Another thing to note is that although you should be simple, your message should be unique to your brand. Don't sacrifice creativity for simplicity.

Location

The location of your CTA directly affects its effectiveness. If you place your call to action in a place that your audience cannot see it, then it will not perform its work as needed.

So, where do you place your CTA on your funnel? Here are some few guidelines that might help:

- If your sales funnel does not have a lot of text, it is better to place your CTA above the fold of your funnel. However, if your funnel has a lot of content, it would make more sense if you placed the CTA below the fold of the funnel.

- You should keep your CTA on the right side of your sales funnel's landing page. This is because people typically read from top to bottom and left to right.

- In the case of mobile devices, it is only logical that you should place your CTA near the top of your page. This is because the audience, in this case, is using lesser screens.

Additional Call to Action Best Practices

Just like with any other marketing strategy, you have to be flexible. This calls for you to continually test the wordings of your CTA so as to find out what resonates better with your target audience.

For this, I usually use ClickFunnels which helps with split testing. Split testing, in this case, helps you try out different calls to action and thus determine which yields a higher result.

In addition to the wording, you should also check out for the graphics that you use for your CTA. Your call to action button should stand out from the rest of the content. This is by use of maybe a bigger button or a contrasting color from that of the background.

With all these done, you will surely be on your way to higher conversion rates with your sales funnel.

Chapter 12: Plan for Generating Traffic

It is of no doubt that Facebook is the leading social media platform nowadays. It has held on to its supremacy for some several years now.

Facebook initially started as a pure social media platform where friends and family would connect. However, over time, it has evolved to be an effective medium for promoting brands and marketing businesses.

How Has This Happened?

The goal of most marketers is usually to reach their potential customers. With the way Facebook started to connect people together, it was not long before marketers identified its marketing potential. In addition to this, Facebook provided a platform where businesses could create their own pages.

It is for this reason that Facebook has become the go-to social network when it comes to advertising and lead generation. For this to happen, you will need to create a successful Facebook advertising funnel. This can be a bit tedious and expensive. However, with a platform like ClickFunnels, all this work can be greatly reduced. This is because all you will have to do is to sync your sales funnel on ClickFunnels with your Facebook page and you are set to go!

So, how can Facebook be of benefit to your business?

Benefits of Facebook Marketing for a Business

Massive Exposure on Global Scale

With over 1.2 billion user accounts, Facebook is undoubtedly the big daddy of social media. This means that by using Facebook alone, you are selling your product to over a billion people worldwide. That is definitely a large audience.

In addition to the large audience, Facebook provides multiple platforms for marketing. This is in the form of pages, groups, and also ads (Jhajharia, 2018).

Facebook pages are usually the most common way of representing individuals or even businesses.

Facebook groups, on the other hand, are usually opened

mostly by businesses or organizations so as to promote their activities. Users are usually allowed to join these groups and can also post comments on the group page called a wall.

Lastly, Facebook ads can be used by businesses which want to target users with extremely specific demographics usually selected by the advertiser.

Low Marketing Expenses

For any business, capturing the largest audience is the main marketing objective. In these days, the online way is the best way to use so as to achieve that goal. This will thus call for you, as an entrepreneur, to have a website. Websites, however, usually cost money to develop, host, and maintain. This can be a great challenge for small businesses.

This, therefore, leaves you with just one option, Facebook. Facebook is a platform that any business can use to market its product. This is because it is free of cost.

Take, for example, creating a Facebook page, you can create one free of any cost, and you can also upload anything on this page. Then, there are Facebook ads. These are quite budget friendly too. The ads are usually charged on a different basis depending upon what suits you.

Some of the popular charging methods are the CPM (Cost per Million) and the CPC (Cost per Click). The CPM is charged per thousand impressions while the CPC is charged per click.

Ability to Target Potential Customers

Facebook is a networking platform that is used all over the world. This large audience can sometimes be a problem when you only want to interact with a certain group of the audience.

It is for this reason that Facebook usually has the Facebook ads feature. This feature helps you target potential customers based on their demographics and interests. For example, if you want to advertise for men clothing, you could target men aged 20 to 35.

In addition to this, Facebook also enables re-targeting those visitors who had earlier visited your site, thus effectively narrowing down your target audience.

Increasing Your Web Traffic

For the increased connection between a business and the users, Facebook provides links which guide the users to the website of your business. Once on your landing pages, the users can now be exposed to more direct marketing pitch in the form of call to action. This will make it easy for you as an entrepreneur to reach a larger audience.

Facebook also goes a step further to provide a feature that enables the users that like your page, start receiving any updates that you make on your Facebook page. In fact, even their friends can see the updates and posts. This makes Facebook's reach a lot bigger.

Useful Info – Facebook Insights and Competitor Information

For every post you upload on Facebook, there is a large number of people who can get to see and interact with it. Facebook usually breaks down these numbers for you and provides them in a way that is easily digestible.

For example, for a Facebook ad, Facebook usually displays the data on the number of page likes, total reach of your post, and also the number of people that engaged with the post. Some useful data about individual post's performance is also made available.

Facebook also has a feature called the Facebook Adverts Manager that lets you track a range of performance metrics. These will help in measuring the impressions (number of times the ad was shown), reach (number of people who saw your ad), and frequency (number of times visitors go through your ad).

Conclusion

Finally, Facebook is the best online platform that you can rely on. This is because it is just the complete package. Low costs, large audience, multiple platforms for marketing, what else can you really ask for.

However, for you to reap the most out of Facebook, you have to build a successful Facebook advertising funnel. By use of ClickFunnels, all this work of creating one from scratch can be greatly reduced. This is because all you will have to do is sync your sales funnel on your ClickFunnel with your Facebook page.

Make the smart move!

Chapter 13: Why Paid Traffic Is King

Paying for traffic has become a powerful tool for all marketers who have been utilizing it. Almost half of the small to medium businesses that have gone online always consider the social media as one of the effective marketing places to venture in using the relevant ads. It does better than a long email list or the site itself.

If you are considering Facebook as one of the places to pay, that's good, but there are numerous platforms out there to try out. In ClickFunnels, they offer their services by first trying their platform, but it's about $100 per month to actually realize what they can do for you. By paying ClickFunnels to help you conduct online business, that is a sure way to generate traffic to the funnels you construct in there.

If you are looking for more traffic, some of the big sources to check include:

- Display adverts such as those appearing on the side of web pages. Of late, they are erased by the ad blocker.

- Paid searches like what Google AdWords offer

- Social media ads such as sponsored adverts on Facebook, Twitter, and Instagram or on

YouTube before the main video plays.

- Influencers promoting your product on various online platforms.

- Sponsored content on websites or magazines that looks like you are sponsoring a particular brand.

As you pay for the marketing services to increase traffic, you could be looking for various options such as PPC (Pay per Click), PPA (Pay per Acquisition), PPV (Pay per View), or just a flat rate for services such as paying a certain amount of fee when you reach a specified target.

With all the options out there that you can explore, you need to check what works for before venturing. Mixing up the paid traffic with the usual customer generation have made businesses to go places. As you look for what you need to pay for, here are some of those that you can consider, and you will see why you should consider them.

Google AdWords

They are considered as something of the past for marketers, but it is still one of the huge traffic sources. We all know Google and who else knows it. On the other hand, reaching all these people means paying more for the cost per click. The idea here is to choose carefully the keywords that your prospects will use to search and then bid an ad using them so that they appear as one of the first search results – at the top of the page.

Since AdWords has gone through tremendous changes as we progress, you can use the dynamic search ads feature to customize your advert on your website content and what people are searching. That way, you don't have to play with keywords whenever you need a Google ad.

AdWords offer you a chance to adjust your bids depending on the device, target users in a certain location or based on demography and also retargeting people who have visited your website before (Ference, 2017). If you are more specific on your targets using AdWords, you increase your chances of winning in the end. Before you figure out what works for your brand, you will need to experiment and keep records on the changes that have brought a positive effect.

Although most of the people ignore ads from Google, the Google Display Network (GDN) can put you out there, so it is also something that you can try out. Yes, people will ignore you, but you cannot reject the fact that GDN reaches about 90% of the people visiting the internet.

In summary,

- AdWords offer the potential to reach a larger audience and also remarket. It is essential to test and see what works for your brand.

- If you find success in using AdWords, then thank the Google Display for the good work.

Facebook Adverts

Every business is going to Facebook to showcase their products and services, so there is every reason to go there. There are tons of people using Facebook and reaching them may require you to try the advertising feature for $5 and see what happens.

Of late, Facebook is facing changes which means you can choose where you want your ads to appear. Choices include the newsfeed, the messenger, or public. You can also target people by specifying the location, interests, age bracket, and occupation among other aspects.

When it comes to designing the adverts, you can choose to use text, images, slideshows, or a video. The good thing about paying for Facebook ads is that you can specify whom you want to reach out and what exactly you want them to hear from you. Your campaign can be dynamic, small, big or looking forward to retarget former customers. Whatever you need to do on Facebook, it's now doable and cashing out means a lot of people will see you.

Other options may involve using Facebook lead ads which allow people to give you their contact information or having links leading to your website. There is so much to see and learn here, and there are resources to help you manage the best practices if you are not yet an expert in making the best out of paid advertisements.

In summary,

- There are a lot of options to try out once you pay for an advert on Facebook.

- You need to learn what will work for you on your way to success.

- If you don't know what you are doing, seek help.

LinkedIn Adverts

If you are in the B2B niche, using native ads on LinkedIn is another way to pay for traffic. You can target your former customers or visitors by their contact, account, title, industry, or geographic location. As for advert options, you can make use of the display advertisement, sponsoring a post on the main feed or using InMail adverts.

You can also get contact forms to fill just like in Facebook lead ads, but the greater advantage of using LinkedIn is to target specific people by using their business or career information. You see, LinkedIn is all about professionals, which implies that they will reach for adverts and read them in a 'different' way. If you have such a mindset and want to explore that form of advertising, LinkedIn ads and relevant sources for the best practices will help you do that.

LinkedIn is, however, expensive since the cost per click is around $2 and more targeting starts at $4.50.

In summary,

- LinkedIn is for you if you want results in the B2B niche, the educated, or recruits

- It is expensive but definitely worth the effort.

Twitter Adverts

It is somehow interesting to join Twitter because only those who are good in it get conversions. You can always do it using the organic way (no payment) but people are always wary of adverts from brands on Twitter, and they will compare you a lot as part of Twitter and its culture. Untimely tweets are known to blow on people's faces, and you don't want to get people giving a mixed feeling about it. You need to understand the Twitter realm and how people go about their business for you to convert customers to buyers.

When done right, the conversions here are massive. According to Twitter statistics, about 94% of customers on Twitter plan to purchase something from the upcoming business they are currently following. 69% of the customers have actually bought something they saw on Twitter. That is why you need to consider paying for ads on Twitter.

You can pay for a single tweet, your account, follow video view, or leads among others. You can also choose your audience using geographic location, gender, or interests. Twitter has made businesses realize more conversions when they promote strong CTAs.

In summary,

- You can get more followers for free if you have something they need

- There are amazing conversions when you pay for adverts as an upcoming brand

Concluding the Chapter

There is a lot of variation when it comes to paid advertising but mixing it with organic methods is a proven way to increase the number of customers flowing down your funnel. You need to build trust at first before you pay and ask for something in return from your customers. Overall, when spending money for something worthy to customers and you believe in it, the grass is always greener on the other side.

Chapter 14: Why Your Fear of Spending Money on Marketing Is False

Deciding that you will be spending money on a sales funnel program like I did and other things such as advertising need a reason to do so. You just don't wake up and decide, and that is a reason to make you live in constant fear as your business struggles to get on its feet. Facing the fact that the checks will always fluctuate as the sales do is not something that many would settle for. Many people are diving into untried waters of entrepreneurship every day. Still, most of them will quit or close the business since their plan was not sufficient or they didn't plan at all. Others, it's due to lack of proper funding.

It is easy to solve the planning problem, but financial situations demand sacrifice and commitment since it's not easy. You may have access to financial support, but you also need to have the right mind when spending it. Are you capable of hoarding or do you spend as it comes? Are you willing to spend extra cash when you need to? Are you worried about spending too much money or managing what you have?

Today, businesses are bound to fail due to the following:

- They do not want to spend on social media channels for advertising purposes. That limits their exposure.

- Not spending money on development of new content, products, and services to supply to potential customers

- Not improving or spending to learn new skills in your business

- Your website is not up-to-standards since you spent less on overall quality and imagery

- Not investing in programs that allow you to simplify your work or make it better.

The sad truth about our financial situations is that they will always stress you as you progress. The pressure of handling money affects how our businesses thrive every day. You can say that you can't afford something that has the potential of pushing your business to the next level, but you do have a vacation already set.

Sacrificing something for a better future gives you two things:

- Success in future when everything goes as planned or you have a gradual increase

- In the steps you fail or that demand you to do better, you will learn what is expected of you

Shifting your mind is not easy, and you might want to stay out of it, but it is necessary if you are seeking to grow. If you are not yet in a position to fund your financial strategy, then you can consider it as a side hustle until things get better. Taking your time is essential when things are tight.

Success and prosperity need you to overcome what you are fearing and start making room for your budget and personal life. Commitment on both ends will achieve a better result if you plan and stick to it. Of late, I have seen a need to increase my advertising budget on ClickFunnels, which means I may even need to expand my account since I deal with a number of products. Also, with the way the customers are calling every day, the question of expanding my space is hitting me harder which mean I need to consider that. If I have to cut out my spending for the business to flourish, so be it.

Are you willing to give up your fear and focus on what your business needs to thrive?

Why Do You Need To Spend Money On Marketing?

Your Message Means Something

Since you want to convert potential customers, then it means you have something to give in return. So, how will they know about your business and what it stands for if you don't fund the necessary channels to express yourself? You need to use the available means of communication to market and share your message. At times, you may need to introduce yourself online for people to know you and what you are doing before they know how to get you. That saves time when people are consulting you for the first time.

You Are Approving Of Being Legitimate

Everyone out there will judge you by the looks. If you are not present on the online end, people might not recognize your efforts. Statistics show that about 95% of customers search online for the products or services they need. When you invest in marketing services, people get the notion that you are succeeding in what you do. They will, therefore, search for you to get more information. Apart from that, they will know that your brand truly exists.

There Is a Crowd on the Internet

A lot of businesses are increasing their online presence just like millions of customers are streaming. A lot of products and services are being advertised, and there is aggressive competition on the rise. How will people get to know you if you don't invest in compelling marketing services? You need to be on multiple channels, doing different things from writing blogs to participating in online platforms.

Time Is a Limiting Factor for Marketers

There are various options to try out if you want to cut down on your marketing efforts. If you know how to work on a good website, market it on social media, and generate email lists, you can always find a way to get it done cheaply.

Other times, even with all the right tools, you may not know the right direction to take. The reason why I chose a platform like ClickFunnels is that I did not have time to combine a lot of factors that contribute to an effective sales funnel. That way, I was able to fund one platform that can help me work on the best practices under one roof.

Concluding the Chapter

When addressing your fear of marketing, I am not advising you to spend huge chunks on every fancy technology out there in the name of marketing. On the other hand, do not depend on going free of charge on everything you are trying to do. Find a balance between what you want to achieve and what you can afford. Start small with a few strategies, tools, and platforms then see how you will progress as time goes by. It is only after progressing that you will know what to adjust, add, or eliminate until you are satisfied with the results.

Chapter 15: Running Facebook Ads

Facebook has a lot of followers, and that is why businesses are advertising their offers on the platform. You have already seen ads on your newsfeed from the pages you like and people liking and commenting about them. Due to the masses in there, businesses are taking social media advertising seriously, and the rewards are huge.

It is cheap to launch a Facebook ad, and you can always track the success by watching how you are performing on your page. Since you can also optimize it, Facebook gives you control over how you want your advert to be, but that also means that you need to know what you are doing. There are businesses that have already succeeded while others have just wasted money.

If you have a small and upcoming business that seeks to increase online sales, this is what I want you to picture at the back of your mind. There is an e-commerce store that made $1500 with 152 purchases from Facebook after spending $500 on the ads. Based on the money spent, the owner used $3.4 to buy each customer.

Does that sound like a good business for you? If it does, then you might want to practice and see where it gets you. I use my sales funnel to reach out to people on social media, and one thing I have learned is that Facebook is a must if you want to get viral out there.

How to Run Facebook Ads

Here are some of the points to note as you prepare to run your ad campaign on Facebook.

Your Goal as Your First Lead

Before you run a Facebook ad, you need to know what you want out of the advertisement. Some people will want followers, others more engagement, or increasing sales conversion. Whatever you want to achieve, Facebook can make that happen.

On Facebook, you have an option to select the marketing objectives that match with what you want to achieve. If you want more visitors to your website, a traffic campaign will be good for you. If you are looking for more sales, then conduct a conversion campaign. As you select your objectives, some of them have subcategories. That means you can specify more on how you want to advertise your business.

Your end goal may not match how Facebook can customize your ad, but it is always close to what you need for your business. Whether you need conference attendance or people to register for downloads, Facebook will help do exactly that.

For you, just have a clear goal in mind that will determine how your ads will perform.

Point Out Your Audience

With 1.28 billion users on Facebook every day, you have the potential of converting a chunk of the population to customers for your online sales. Companies and individuals now have Facebook pages which means you have a wide variety to choose from.

With such an analysis, you cannot just post anything on Facebook and expect some sales conversions. You have to run an ad campaign that is successful enough to convince the masses. Facebook gives you options on where to start.

You can choose to start by selecting the cold audience which involves everyone on Facebook or what you are already familiar with – the followers on your page or a customized audience. If you already have a number of followers that you can work with, then you can work on turning them into customers. This makes your ad familiar to people who already know your page and business and are interested in what you are offering.

You may not have too many followers, but your business may have collected some contact information. You can use the generated customer list to create a custom audience. Facebook gives you an option of uploading the list before generating an audience that matches the users you have issued. Now, most businesses, when starting, they don't have too many followers, and they may not have a reliable customer list. If that is your case, then start building your audience by using the 'Everyone' option.

When it comes to narrowing your audience, it can be quite cumbersome, but the Facebook Audience Insights tool can be of service to you. Here, you start by specifying some parameters which may include targeting people from a certain location and in a specific age group among other options. After setting your target audience parameters, you can start looking for data related to followers on competitor pages.

That will give you a better position to start targeting. The information you get from your competitors are reports collected by Facebook and third-party partners' collaboration. The information can be useful later when you want to perform A/B or split testing to determine which ads will work for the good of your business.

Use of Breath-Taking Images

A picture says more about your business than just pure content. That is why your competitors are using images that you have never seen before to capture their audience attention. Most Facebook users are there to watch what is happening around them and what their friends are up to. Therefore, if you don't have an eye-catching image on your ad, then users will just scroll down the newsfeed to watch a video about a friend's birthday party.

To prevent customers from passing your ad, using clear and quality images is no exception. If you don't have a good camera, it is time to invest in one or hire a professional to do it for you. Before uploading your images, make sure your editing incorporates not more than 20% of text content. More content makes Facebook show your ad to fewer users. One more thing, make your images relevant to your business.

Since Facebook is also accepting video content, why don't you shoot one and upload it there? A video can talk more about your business and offers more than what an image can do. With an auto-play feature, you can capture users' attention as they scroll. Just make sure you utilize the mute feature since most videos are actually watched that way.

Either way, a video or image will help you run a

successful ad campaign, but they all have to clear and bright for the view. One tip is using people's faces since our brains work better at face recognition. If you have an image of a person using your product or service, that's much better.

Do You Know What To Say?

The first three points will enable you to run an ad campaign on Facebook. However, you need to add a message that tells people more about your products or services. As you write down your message, you need to consider the following elements: a headline that grabs user attention, a phrase that adds weight to your ad, and a call to action.

More customer conversion requires your ad to have buzzwords such as 'free' or 'Promo code.' If you are running a deal, you can make people hurry up and click more by using words like 'You Have 24 Hours to Grab This Deal' or 'Act Fast!' People will fear that they may run out of time and miss out. So, they will join you as soon as they see your ad. If you advert is not urgent, then words like 'See it Yourself' or 'Test' will work to create a form of urgency.

If you already know what to say, then it's time to focus on what you shouldn't say. Facebook is sometimes watchful on ads that use the word 'You' and they may not allow such ads to run. You can, however, tackle that by saying 'Your' or 'You're' in the ads. Also, make sure that whatever you are advertising is allowed since products such as firearms cannot be advertised. Otherwise, flagging will occur.

Don't Advertise Like an Advertisement

Studies have shown that people don't like ads that actually sound like adverts. If you are persuading people through your Facebook ads, people are more likely to reject you. This point might make you feel like there is no point of advertising, but people will not like it if you indeed sound like you are advertising.

The motive here is to make people understand why they need to join you or buy from you. If they know the benefits of clicking your call to action, that will make you gain more followers than actually advertising your offers. It's a common thing for people not liking to be told what to do. Therefore, talk about what they will benefit from once they join you or follow your CTA.

Make Use of Split Testing

We have talked about split testing in chapter 10 and what it's all about. You can apply the techniques on Facebook advertising campaign to know which ads will perform well on your page.

Here, it's all about creating different variations of your main ad and testing those variations on divided segments of your audience to see which one works better at delivering information. It can also be used to test various parts of your ad so that you can arrive at the best combination of the final advert.

You can start with two images and two copies. The variation should create 4 ads in total for the test. After testing them against each other, you can now combine the best image and copy combination before testing other elements such as headlines and buttons. Split testing takes time (days to be specific), but you will see its worth in the end.

Use Conversion Pixels

It is a useful tool that will help you run your ads on Facebook. A pixel here is a small code section that you can use on your website to track the conversions and retarget using your leads. It also collects useful data that you can use to customize your ad for the target audience.

Installing Facebook pixels will help you analyze how people see and react to your ads and the sales funnel you are creating. You can see what people clicked so as to get to your website and the pages they clicked once they landed there. You can also get to know which device they used to reach you.

Using such information will help to know which ads are working to your benefit, and what you need to adjust or get rid of for more conversions. If people are reaching you more on mobile than computers, you can work on your ad to favor the PDA users.

Connect Your Ads to Your Landing Page

In chapter 8, we talked about how you can create a great landing page. If you are running an ad campaign on Facebook, it then makes sense to connect your ads to your landing page for more conversions. Once users click on it and go straight to the page, that will increase your chances of generating more sales and enlarging your customer base.

Running Facebook ads is essential today, but you also need to invest your time, money, and resources to realize more customer conversions. Once you your plan and goal are clear, the rest is all about putting the right thing in the right place. ClickFunnels has enabled me to reach out for more customers and using Facebook ads has helped me retarget them and enlarge my conversion rate. I also use Facebook ads to introduce a new product I'm willing to sell and collect user views about it. That aids me in strategizing on what I should add or leave out in my sales business.

Chapter 16: Email Lists and Why You Need One

Today, businesses are focusing more on social media than emails when it comes to online marketing. On the other hand, if you are continually building your sales funnel like me, email contacts still remain an integral part of your marketing strategy. So, it is not that primitive like some advisors would tell you.

If you want your customers to thoroughly understand your products or services, sending them emails about it will help them get all the relevant information. It also means that the customers you convert will join you with an informed decision. Even in social media, every platform requires you to have an email address. So, it is still a winner here.

Statistics show that email marketing yields higher results on ROI (Return on Investment) than social media. That is why we are going to talk about it in this chapter. So that you can conduct an email marketing campaign, it is essential for you to grow an email list. I had earlier introduced email lists in chapter 4 when discussing why you need a strong pipeline. Here is an insight about them which includes tips on how to grow one.

What an Email List Entails

It is simply a list of email addresses that you send information to on a daily or weekly basis depending on your scheduling. When it comes to marketing, email lists are used to distribute information about products and services offered among other updates by a business. If you are subscribed to news or information that comes via your email, it means that you have been included in the provider's email list. That is how it works.

In ClickFunnels, you can build an email list that you can use to promote your sales funnel by sending emails about new products, webinars, or to collect views about something you want to launch. Whatever it is your funnel is doing, ClickFunnels can help you collect the emails and schedule them for newsletters and information about what you need them to know.

If you already have a website that you would like people to join, there are email marketing programs out there that can help you collect organize the email addresses you collect so that you can automate sending general content or customize the content that suits a particular group among other capabilities.

Why Small Businesses Need To Grow Their Email List

As you are starting out, you need an audience that will help you launch successfully and move forward. So, you launch your first product or service, and people are there to receive you. You set up an event and people trickle in to enjoy. As you open the doors the next morning and thereafter, people will know that they are not alone.

Your phone rings every time somebody visits your website which means traffic is growing on that end. Now, if all these people are coming and you don't have something to make them feel connected and stay with you when they are out there, then you are not working on building a relationship with them. If they feel connected to you by sending them information about what you are up to, then that will drive them to act more and bring in revenue to your business.

You Can't Rely On Social Media Alone

You have the opportunity of running Facebook ads as discussed in the last chapter or opening accounts in other social media platforms. Yet, unless you are leading them to your landing page or the sales funnel platform, you don't actually own any of their contacts.

Growing an email list enables you to take charge of the messages you deliver and how you communicate to your target audience. Since you have people that you can contact, you have the ability to talk to the only people who are interested in buying your products or services and attending your events. By sending them information directly to their inbox, you give them an opportunity to opt-in first hand and receive information customized for them and only them.

Therefore, using an email list is the best way to convert your subscribers to customers and members of your sales society.

Why You Need To Grow Your Email List

Once you understand what an email list can do for you, then there is a need to keep it growing. As the list enlarges, you increase the likelihood of your target audience receiving your offers and other general information. More emails mean that more people are getting to know you out there and those already in there can be retargeted for future transactions. That way, word is spreading that you actually exist.

A continuous growth on your email list allows you to keep the cycle active and the more prospects are receiving more information from you, the more you increase your opportunities when they contact you.

You Can Do More with an Email List

After attaining an email list that is continually growing, you can start to see how you can engage your audience differently. At times, it is not always about contacting your customers about new offers or promoting something you know they should have. Since you will always get a response, you will start to see what people are actually vying for and what they want. At that point, you can address them individually by focusing on their needs. That will be different from how you contact the larger population.

Once you keep track of how you interact with the emails, you can understand what people are facing and what they are looking forward to solve. If you center the business in a way that you will be addressing these problems, you will know the right content to send them, so that they can make an informed purchase or follow your lead.

Since not all businesses fetch information about their customers, you can take that as an advantage over your substitutes who don't rely on keeping their customer contacts.

Tips on Building Your Email List

Start Soon

This is not generally a requirement but some advice to take. For you to be effective at building your email list, your vision should lay ground as soon as you realize it so that you can spend more time working on it. The earlier you start, the earlier you get to work and build your plan.

Start With Those with You

As you start to grow your list, it is essential to start with the emails you already have. If you have emails from the previous marketing campaign, you can include that in the current CRM. If not, then you need to start looking for contacts.

Build an Incredible Blog

Your email list will be feeding on information for the

subscribers to learn and purchase your products or services. Therefore, blogs will bring them in, educate the prospects about what you are doing, and also get a chance to join you via the call to actions that you have created.

Content takes time to develop but eventually, it's worth it. As you move forward, create calls for people to subscribe to your emails or join your events if you have one. When getting their information, a name and email address are enough. Do not ask for more than that if you are starting out.

Consider Having an Opt-In

In chapter 7, we talked about a lead magnet. There are those people who will not give out their information unless they are getting something valuable in return. As you continue building content, offer something that will make people subscribe to you. If you still have no idea, revisit the chapter to see how you can do that.

Add a Sharing Option

When you add a share feature on your email newsletters and blogs, you set a powerful way of your subscribers to distribute the information to other viewers on the internet. If your customer posts a coupon from your business or shares something worth considering, those who view your customer will see it. If what they posted made them feel good and satisfied with your business, the friends to your customer will incline towards you. That is how you get future followers.

The most important thing here is for you to offer something valuable.

Concluding the Chapter

If you have difficulty in building an email list, there are dozens of platforms to help you do so. ClickFunnels has a built-in feature that helps you create and grow your email list. You can customize and schedule your blogs as you wish here, and it also offers a room for split testing when you want to test for new products and services.

Chapter 17: Email Drip Campaigns and How to Build Them

Email drip campaigns are primarily aimed at attracting subscribers that can commit to your call to action. Bombarding subscribers with emails that may not interest them tends to have a negative effect on the intended results. The audience holds all the cards in today's marketing field. Hence the topics may need to be custom made for them.

It is important to achieve a balance between building a subscriber's list and keeping them engaged. An email drip campaign helps in sustaining your email marketing strategy.

Automated email marketing campaigns involve sending prewritten marketing information through emails to prospective customers in a verge to direct them towards an aimed conversion point. They are called "drip" campaigns as they are done over an extended period, slowly providing valuable pieces of information to your subscribers on updates, new products, and notifications that may interest them.

Example:

Email drip campaigns are automated based on set

timelines or a subscriber's actions or inactions. For instance, emails may be set to be sent out immediately a user subscribes to your mailing list and for the subsequent ten weeks on a set day of the week. On another instance, a user visiting an upgrade page for a while without actually upgrading could be set to receive a drip email to explain further on the upside of upgrading.

In other words, drip campaigns are used to deliver crucial information to the subscriber at the right moment to tip them to conversion by pushing them down your click funnel.

How to Set Up a Drip Campaign

Identify Your Target Audience

Successful drip campaigns usually target information to a select set of customers by breaking down your subscriber's list into groups. It is crucial to identify the groups and triggers to use in the strategy for your drip campaign.

Drip campaigns are mostly based on two modes of triggers. Usually, they are either added user demographic information or custom actions in your website or app (Stych, n.d.).

Tracking user behavior is the best way to customize email marketing campaigns in order to send needed information to users at the right moment. Is the user a loyal customer? How often do they shop? What are they looking for in your store? Is it a bargain or a particular brand? How often do they login?

Determine the problem you solve for your customers. This way your drip campaigns are more effective as they targeted to certain behaviors.

You should base your drip campaign on audience characteristics such as how often they visit your website, how long they have been subscribers, how likely they are to click on content subjects in your newsletter, their frequency on your premium service pages, or how long they have been customers.

Craft Your Message

Once you have identified your target audience, it is important to generate a helpful message that captures the user's attention. What action do you intend the user to take? Or what information you aim to pass to the user.

Using these questions as a guide, write a clear, actionable, and attractive message. Don't compromise the voice of your brand but maintain clarity in your message.

Plan Out Your Campaign

Figure out the workflow of your whole campaign from first contact, support to users, and sales. Meanwhile, your campaign should have a set of goals with a well-planned strategy of quantifying your results.

You could answer the set of questions below to achieve this:

1) How many emails should I send, when and in what order?

The sequence in which you send out emails to a new user plays an important role in engaging the user and keeping their attention. It is crucial for you to consider the timing of the emails, the amount of information and reasons the user might require this information.

2) Do the triggers align with my message?

Emails received by users should always be applicable to them at that moment. It's annoying to get an email coupon for a product already purchased, or a detailed sales pitch email immediately after signing up. Each drip campaign email should correspond to the trigger as laid out.

3) How do I measure my success?

At this stage, the reason behind setting up the drip campaign is already determined. They can vary from acquiring customers, engaging subscribers to educate them of newly released products and updates. You can choose the means to measure your progress against a predetermined set of goals. Consider the bounce rate, click-through rate, conversions or time on site. The means of measurements determined should always reflect the reason behind your campaign.

Start Your Campaign

Start sending out your messages immediately after devising a strategy for your campaign. You can purchase an off-the-shelf product to have you running in a matter of minutes or you could come up with a custom drip software.

Evaluate and Adjust

Supervision is required even though your drip

campaign is automated. Your strategy and user subsections should be readjusted based on the results you want to achieve. You could rewrite your custom actions to achieve the frequency of click-throughs you are aiming for. Increase the educational aspect of your sale-closing email for them to achieve their desired conversion rate when asking the user to pull the trigger. Keep evaluating, adjust accordingly and repeat the cycle.

Concluding the Chapter

In conclusion, you may need to understand what an email drip campaign is in order to achieve the best results. It not only involves prewritten emails, but they are sent out over a pre-set timeline usually following certain triggers in your website. You do not have to set it up from scratch. You can purchase an automated drip campaign to avoid the hustle of having to learn how to do it. The steps in setting up a drip campaign are; identify your target audience, write your message, have a well laid out plan for your campaign, begin your campaign, and lastly evaluate the progress and adjust accordingly.

Chapter 18: Plan on Engaging Your Audience

Coming up with engaging content is as important as coming up with enough content in marketing. Engaging content creates traffic for your site by keeping them hooked on your content. It's not as easy as it sounds.

Users will only be interested if your content is what they need. Providing the right content to the right people at the right time is vital to keeping your audience engaged. It should not only be good but appealing to people's pains or pleasures. As a marketing strategy, it is important to know what your target audience is looking for. Make their life easier by solving one of their problems and win over their hearts.

How to Boost Engagement

In your sales funnel, engagement is usually at the top and middle of it. Therefore, engagement strategies such as discounts, and promotions attract repeat and new traffic. Engagement mainly requires retaining quality and standing out from the crowd of newsfeeds. This can prove to be a challenge even for the best of us. Here are some pointers to customer engagement and also re-engagement.

Acquire a Deep Understanding of Your Platforms

In a quest to understand your audience and their behavior, you should understand the platforms they visit and why they visit them. This way you can engage with them better as you know what they are doing in these platforms.

Uniquely designed polls and surveys are a great way to get your audience to offer you crucial information. Email newsletters can be coupled with quizzes in order to collect data for both engagement and re-engagement. If you aim at re-engaging, it is important to switch up the questions to avoid boring your audience.

The motive is not restrained to finding out about the audience but also to register the sense of when (in real time) and how they engage. Knowing when and how the audience answers polls can be as informative as the answers themselves.

Micro-Moments Matter

Basically, micro-moments are the defining touchpoints

to every stage in the decision making process that lead to the purchase. Nowadays, people are quick to make a decision, and they do not tend to be location-based.

Businesses are being caught off guard in capturing consumers' decisions in the moment. This is driving businesses to make fast decisions on products without much thought over the motivation behind the customers purchasing decisions. You could get ahead of this by addressing customer needs by optimizing content through queries.

Bounce rates (window shopping) may give you an idea of how consumers behave, such as when they compare prices to your competitors before making a purchase. Don't forget to pay close attention to mobile-based numbers to fully grasp the intensity of micro-moment actions as they happen.

Use Customer Data Tracking Strategies

Re-engagement trickles down to dedicating your attention from the first round of customers. Getting subscribers for your newsletters and enrolling them into programs gives you a sense of their desires and needs. This allows you to brush on possible strategies for re-engagement.

This should not be dependent on making sales but

actually about making the user interacting with your business have a valuable experience. It could be as simple as setting up a 'points' card'. The opportunity for a reward without spending a lot of money as they experience your site could prove incentive enough.

Understanding your customer's journey step by step may shine some light on a leak in your sales funnel. When tracking your customers' data, you are able to re-engage previous visitors and engage new traffic hence rectify any fall in traffic.

Be Consistent and Retain Value

Trust gained through consistency retains engagement by maintaining brand loyalty and awareness. Maintain consistency in your marketing plan. Engage your audience with complementary activities and while offering them valuable incentives.

Offer important information regularly, as consistency is key. Blogging on a regular basis keeps your audience in the loop for valuable information. Remember to share this on your channels.

You must strive to be ahead of your competitors even in your informational value. Go a step further when providing a service or a product to your audience. For instance, instead of providing your target audience with just tips why not go on to link them to other resources or free tools designed by you.

Focus On Segmentation

When planning for your drip marketing campaign, start off on targets basing on different audience segments. Certain demographics are likely to impact on your overall strategy.

Concentrate on the customer segments that are most valuable. This entails customers that can return and that are likely to spend money. Group your customers according to channels, such as purchases that are made via your mobile app.

Target realistic and specific goals that are in line with the promotion of your business. They should be focused on measurable performance indicators going beyond your profit. This, however, should not make you set unrealistic targets. Your goals must be set with a timeline and should have accessible points set in line with your marketing strategies.

Re-Target To Re-Engage

Don't get comfortable when you register high traffic. Apply digital marketing retargeting as a means of keeping your audience engaged. Consider acquiring display ads for previous audience or customers.

Consider the following pointers in retargeting:

- Focus on traffic to specific webpages. Identify your audience's interests in order to know what they want and deliver personalized information to them.

- Offer different ads. Maintain the look on the ads but make sure you have varying formats or sizes. This increases the chances of capturing your audience attention.

- Consider setting up retargeting pixel as part of your email signature. Follow the pixel depending on the group of subscribers that opened them. This ensures you identify the interested parties to your product.

When re-targeting to re-engage, avoid coming out as overzealous, as it can be a turn off to your customers. Don't overdo it.

Once you attain a certain following for your business blog or website, it is important to keep the engagement of your target audience. There are certain pointers to boosting your reader's engagement. They are; having a better understanding of social media platforms to give you insights on the readers, paying attention to the micro-moments, employing user data tracking strategies, staying consistent and aiming to provide the best value, focus on segments or groups of readers, strive to re-engage your audience by retargeting your marketing strategy.

Chapter 19: Build Relationships

In the past years, all that was needed to achieve success in the business industry was an attractive product with a great price. However, the business industry nowadays has evolved and it is now a whole new ball game. This is because nowadays, you must build a relationship with your consumers so as to be successful in your venture. This is now where relationship selling comes into play.

Relationship selling is mainly focused on the quality of the relationship built between the buyer and the salesperson. This, therefore, means that when building your sales funnel, you should create it in a way that it nurtures this relationship.

So, as to create such a funnel, a lot of effort is needed. However, with ClickFunnels, it can be a lot simpler. ClickFunnels helps in creating a sales funnel that nurtures your relationship with your consumers in that it has pre-built funnels that have features like:

- An opt-in web page that helps you accumulate email addresses from your consumers

- An email auto-responder that sends out emails to your consumers

In short, ClickFunnels provides all the essential

features that will make it easy for you to communicate with your customers and thus build a good relationship.

To understand better about the role of a sales funnel in relationship building, below is the anatomy of a sales funnel and the role each stage plays in relationship-building.

Stage 1: Awareness

- *Leading status:* They know about your business and what you are offering.

- *Your goal:* Provide something that will bring them back.

So, how do you give them a reason to come back? This is by capturing their interest. This is by maybe letting them get to know you better. Share useful, interesting and relevant content on your company's blog or social media platforms. Start building trust using the shared content.

Trust is the first step towards a customer wanting to buy from you. Without it, you'll fail.

Stage 2: Achieving interest and Evaluation

- *Leading status:* You have their attention and they are now weighing options about your offers.

- *Your goal:* Find out what they consider and what they need to achieve. Show them that you have a solution to what they are finding out.

In this step, you will try and convince the prospects that you can provide whatever they need. To do this, you must get your leads' contact information so that you can begin to form a relationship with them. Once you have their contact details, you can now send them more targeted content. This may include demo videos or even free trials.

You can also go a step further to answer any questions they might have perhaps by setting up a call. This will help because they will now trust you a lot more.

Stage 3: Gaining Trust

- *Leading status:* They like your solution and they would like to try it out.

- *Your goal:* Show them the way to purchase.

At this stage, your lead is now ready to make the big step of purchasing your product. So, make doing so as easy as possible for them. This would be the best time to maybe present positive reviews from past customers or maybe offer free shipping for them.

Stage 4: Action

- *Leading status:* They are about to become paying customers. These people are ready to commit.

- *Your goal:* Seal the deal.

Once your leads have now bought your product, you would want to keep them as your committed customers. This means that you must, therefore, reinforce their confidence in their decision to work with you. Sending them a welcome email with implementation tips for their new product or service can be a good way to keep things flowing.

It Is Vital to Manage Your Sales Funnel Since We Are Living In a Relationship Era

Consumers usually seek positive relationships with the companies they do business with, and how you manage your sales funnel ties directly with how your company is set up to create these positive customer relationships.

Managing Sales Funnel like a Guru

Simplify the Funnel

Keep your sales funnel short. You can do this by maybe removing any blockages and eliminate any extra steps or redundancies in your funnel. Some examples of the blockages can be like:

- Having few shopping options for the customer or poor propagation of the refund policy, making the customer abandon the cart

- Your sales are taking too long to process and that makes the leads to lose interest since there are too many steps to follow

If you are unsure about the step to remove, ask yourself of what value is that step to the sales process. If you have trouble coming up with an answer, you can probably remove it.

Focus On Relationships

As much as building customer relationships is a core part of your business, you should work smart rather than hard so as to achieve that. This is by focusing on the most promising leads than investing in the whole lot.

This can be difficult, but it is part of the journey of making a successful sale. Therefore, set up your sales funnel in a way that it can serve as an automatic selling machine for your business by finding the most qualified leads.

Set Measurable Goals

Set the objectives of your sales funnel. This can be like about the revenue growth, increasing your customer base or even something else altogether.

This will help you easily quantify your sales efforts.

Concluding the chapter

In conclusion, relationship selling is an important factor that you should incorporate when creating a sales funnel. With the help of ClickFunnels, you can create a sales funnel that enables you to nurture your relationship with your consumers. This is because ClickFunnels provides essential features that will enhance your communication with your customers at each step of the sales funnel.

In addition to that, you should learn how to manage your sales funnel. This is because the way you manage your sales funnel determines how your business is set up to create positive relationships with the consumers.

Chapter 20: Become an Authority in Your Area

As an entrepreneur, you sometimes wonder whether there is a method you can use so that for every product your brand sells it is bought by every visitor. Unfortunately, there is no proven method to make this a reality. However, there is something that can help with this. It is called being an authority on a subject.

Being an authority on a subject is all about having the authority on one specific subject. This will make you gain the trust and confidence of your visitors and readers.

What Is The Authority Principle?

More often than not, you are usually likely to be persuaded to complete an action by a person who you view is in a position of power at that moment. For example, you will be forced to stop your car if a police officer asks you to do so unlike when a stranger asks you to do the same thing. This is because you believe that this credible source must have your best interests in mind. Now, this is the power of an authority principle. However, an authority principle does not require a person to hold a position of power like a police officer. It can also come from other cues.

For you to create a sales funnel that builds your authority, you will have to put in some great effort. However, with ClickFunnels, all this workload can be greatly reduced. This is because you can integrate some platforms to your sales funnel on ClickFunnels that will help you with most of the work.

With all this said, the question still remains, how can you use authority on your e-commerce site? Here are some ways that can help with that.

How You Can Become an Authority

Knowledge

This is quite straightforward. You should know about a subject for you to gain the authority on it. Therefore, in your sales funnel, show your knowledge of a subject. This can be through writing your academic credentials and also maybe your experience.

On top of that, be sure to back up your knowledge with third-party sources likes references to studies and also maybe quotes from other authoritative sources.

Provide Free Content

Providing free content can really be a boost in making you gain authority over a subject. However, this content should be related to your main product. This content can be in the form of eBooks, infographics, checklists or any other information that adds value to your audience. By doing this, you will reap a great number of benefits like:

- You will be able to test a product in your market and also measure the results with the first material

- You will build a closer relationship with your audience and also increase your online presence

A thing to note is that although the content is free, it should have quality and should be useful to the consumers.

With the help of ClickFunnels, you can integrate a platform like Kajabi that will allow for file downloads.

Have an Active Presence on Social Media

The social media platforms can be very informative channels that can help you gain the authority on a subject.

To start with, you can start by first determining the social media platform that is used by your persona. Then make strategies for these specific channels. The secret here is to major on some few platforms rather than open accounts on all platforms. This will help you focus and provide quality content on these platforms. You should also keep your channels updated and always communicate with your followers.

With ClickFunnels, you can be able to sync your sales funnel with the social media platform of your choice with just a single click.

Respond To Criticism

With authority comes criticism.

When in authority, there must be some people who must criticize you. These people can be such a nuisance and you might feel the need to ignore them. However, the best way to approach criticism is to face it. Respond to those critics. This is because if people find that you are not responding to them, they might think that you are weak. This can make you lose your status as an authority (Bulygo, 2019).

This does not, however, mean that you should start arguments with your critics. You should respond to them in a timely manner and politely. Do not let criticism go unchecked.

With ClickFunnels, you are provided with a platform that you can use to communicate with your critics. This is because you can integrate a platform like Twilio into ClickFunnels. Twilio will help in making and receiving calls and also sending text messages.

Build Partnerships with Other Websites

By growing together with people, you can go really far with your business. Therefore, find websites that share the same theme as you and partner with them. Offer some of your articles to them and also make some room on your website so that other websites can do the same. By doing this, you strengthen your name in other channels; this will definitely boost your authoritative power.

Always Be Honest

As a person in authority, you should know that your every word is scrutinized by your consumers. Therefore, make sure to provide real data and achievements. If you haven't made any big achievements yet, it is better to provide some small results rather than making up achievements.

Concluding the Chapter

Finally, having the authority on a subject can really be of help to your business. However, the thing with this is that you do not gain authoritative power overnight. It takes a lot of time and you should put in a lot of effort into building a sales funnel that will grow your authoritative power. However, with ClickFunnels, this work can be greatly reduced.

So, stay focused!

Chapter 21: Convert Your Leads

One of the goals when building a sales funnel is to get new leads. In whichever way you get them, they are always important when growing your business. The problem comes in when you need to convert your leads into sales and generate revenue. If you or your team struggles to follow the leads you get online, then you are not doing enough and that means no sales.

When marketing, I measure leads' success by seeing how they are converting in my funnel. If someone calls for an order or downloads a PDF I just advertised, then my leads are working. It can take you several weeks to arrive at such a point and while you are doing so, it's possible to lose interest.

How you follow up on your leads is essential to your growth. A slow follow up will hurt your strategy while a quick one will lead to some sales if you do it right.

How to Convert Leads Into Sales

Leads Cannot Wait

Leads are like fresh flowers; they can't wait until the

next day without proper maintenance. Actually, the level of interest is lost within the first hour after booking. If you don't respond, the customer may have probably found someone better to supply the same thing. That calls for having internal routines that will ensure you handle the leads that come at all times.

If you direct leads to your personal inbox, it might skip you due to an overload or you can forget if you have so much to do. It is, therefore, proper to send your leads to a business or company email where someone else can see them and handle on your behalf. You can use a customer service software where necessary to make sure that you handle every customer who comes in.

Qualify Your Online Leads

Here, you need to categorize your leads into MQL (Marketing Qualified Leads) and SQL (Sales Qualified Leads) if you want to raise the conversion rate (Bendorf, 2019). Everyone in each of the named groups is in a different stage in your sales funnel. That means you need different approaches when dealing with these customers.

If someone just downloaded a free subscription or just joined your channel, then it means they need more information about what you do. Such a person is in the MQL stage. You cannot subject such a customer with hard-selling tactics since they might get worried or bored.

As for SQLs, these are the people who already know you and are ready to meet you or purchase from you. Those are the ones that require your attention as soon as they contact you since you might be closing a deal soon.

If you manage to separate your subscribers into the two groups, you will know where each customer is in relation to your sales funnel. When it comes to engaging them, you will know who needs more information about your brand and who need the sales tactics.

Strategize Your Sales Team to Act Quickly

It is okay if you decide to divide your sales team into two categories. One group will be handling the customers who have already joined you while the rest handles new intakes. While that is of importance, what you need to focus on is how your sales team moves the sales and at what pace. Therefore, the process you create is of utmost importance.

That also applies to all departments in your sales funnel. As you deal with the internal handling, consider the following:

- How do you handle your first contacts? Over the phone or email?

- How do you collect contact information?

- At what point do you consider a lead to have converted into a sale?

- How do you follow up on everyday activity?

Follow Up Your Leads

When you have a new contact and you are not able to reach them, you should not give up at that point. You can try to call them at another time since they could be busy when you tried to reach out the first time.

Increasing your connections even at sales point is also necessary. When calling for a sales transaction, you can ask the customer if you can add them to your email list. That way, you can continue to keep in touch even after selling. At times, using too much of your sales tactics on a customer sounds harsh. On the other hand, following up makes sure that your brand is becoming a household name. That can increase the conversions when the prospects are ready.

Listen To What Prospects Have To Say

As you focus on turning your leads into customers, it is essential to listen to their worries and concerns. At times, it is better when you step out of your goals and attend to what your customer has to say. They could be concerned about an obstacle or something they cannot find.

Listening will help you address what the customer needs, educate on what your brand is about, and how your product can solve the problem.

Use Data to Perform an Analysis

Data helps you to see how your business is performing which means you will be watching how your leads are converting. Use an analytics software to come up with a dashboard that shows how leads are joining your CRM at every sales funnel category. Once you compare the input to the output, then you can know where to deal with the leaks in your funnel. Focusing on the leads that do not convert will increase the likelihood of converting.

ClickFunnels provides you with an analysis page that I view via a large screen to see how the sales are performing. It updates in real time so, I always see who is coming in and how many calls I get every day. It also reflects on the percentage increase or drop in sales. That way, I'm able to generate new ideas and repair where things are not going so well.

Concluding the Chapter

Converting leads into sales is not easy and it will take you days to realize your first conversion if you are new in the business. Take your time, and act fast on every new lead that comes by. When the sales are not converting as expected, having a data collection system will help you to point out which areas need perfection. When you follow the tips above, things will be smooth as you progress.

Chapter 22: You Need a System for Your Sales Funnel

By now, you understand how a sales funnel work and if you still have it in theory, it's time to check what ClickFunnels has in store for you. It is possible to build your sales funnel from scratch but combining your website will all the other services you need for it to be effective is cumbersome.

Sales funnel are supposed to lead your prospects through the buying process and help them make a decision using all the strategies and tactics that I have already talked about in the previous chapters. How much time do you think it will take for you to join every piece and module you need before you start to realize some conversions?

What Makes A Sales Funnel Different From Your Website?

Your website is just a piece of the long puzzle. You cannot start converting prospects into sales by creating a website with some blog posts and end things there. You need a strategy that will arrange your sales conversion into a series of steps with the site as the main basis.

You need to consider how to add links to relevant sources to your blogs, include some actionable CTAs, and an opt-in for those who would like to join your brand. All these are meant to move the prospects from one phase of your sales funnel to the next. You have already seen the steps in a sales funnel and all customers fall into the different categories. They, therefore, need different mechanisms when it comes to addressing their concerns.

Following up your customers requires you to have their contact information. That means you are now considering a long email list that you will use to send them information about your business and the buying process. At the top of the funnel, you are also looking forward to increasing your traffic by using social media platforms. So, you have Facebook and Instagram pages among others to take care of that.

When following up, something like an email list becomes an essential part of your sales funnel. It has a series of steps to consider from when people join your platform to when they are considering to buy from you and also the after-sale services.

With all that, it is, therefore, crucial to construct a sales funnel from one angle view instead of having everything separated and it's only your efforts keeping everything together. A sales funnel will make everything automatic since you are controlling everything from a single point.

Reasons Why You Need a Sales Funnel System

With the above discussion in mind, here is why you need an automated sales funnel:

You Will Be Able To Focus On Your Leads

A sales funnel system will allow you to see the leads you need to work on. Since everything is in the system, you have the time and resources to see which leads are likely to convert instead of chasing the people who are not yet ready. The system lets you add preliminary steps that will allow you to see the best method to interact with your potential customers. That way, you will figure out who wants your products or services and who has not yet made a firm decision.

Organized Customer Sorting

An online sales funnel system will help you rank your

prospects accordingly. It allows you to sort and evaluate where your customers are in the sales funnel. That will help you know who requires your immediate action and who is likely to make a purchase. You will also be in a position to separate new customers and the old ones so that you can concentrate on feeding the new ones with information about what the need to know and do.

A System Will Help You Take Care of Long-Term Leads

If you are in the B2B business, you already know that sales can take time before you get a suitable buyer. Since you need consistency in your efforts, a sales funnel will help you to build that so that your engagement period is smooth as you seek to convert. In short, a sales funnel will help you nurture your leads by having a way to follow up until you arrive at the buying phase.

Attract Leads That Will Help You Grow Your Business

Once you work on your sales funnel with the right content among other things that will help you convert, a sales funnel attracts leads that concur with your business goals. Today's world is filled with competitors and new businesses all trying to make something out of themselves. Since it is hard to follow every lead that comes to your way, a sales funnel will help you to focus on only the leads that are likely to convert. It also means you are in a position to speak to your leads directly and address the problem at hand.

Furthermore, you only need leads that will work for you and not every lead out there.

Sales Funnel Helps You Collect Useful Data

Lastly, a sales funnel system will aid in collecting information about how your sales are performing. On one end, you are receiving customers while on the other, there are those who will end up buying from you and others will not. The number of customers you convert is crucial in knowing your position when it comes to the amount of sales generated. All that data is available if you have a system for it.

The data will help you seal the leaks in your sales pipeline and also form a working relationship with your closest customers. It will also help you make informed predictions about the future of your business.

Conclusion: All the Funnel Websites and Why I Believe ClickFunnels Is the Best and Most Robust One

Before I arrived at the notion of creating a sales funnel, my business was at its worst and it was hard to convince customers to buy. By reading this book up to this point, it is clear that building a sales funnel on your own is the hardest thing to do if you don't have a supportive platform to help you achieve higher heights in online sales.

By the time I was joining ClickFunnels, my friends had already recommended some of the best platforms to join. Places like MailChimp and Builderail have gained a good reputation in aiding businesses convert customers into sales. It is after joining ClickFunnels that I realized the potential of a sales funnel and how it can transform your business.

To break it down for you, it is a platform that will let you sell anything from physical products to an online course. That means you already have an alternative to building your own site, landing pages and having to consider all the plugins you need to make it work. ClickFunnels give you an e-commerce site that will allow you to sell by making multi-level pages for selling and issue offers that relate to your funnel.

If you were to build a sales funnel, here is what you would budget for:

- A website costing not less than $3000 depending on how you need it customized for your business

- Adding a shopping cart that will cost more than $30 to set up

- Web hosting services with a minimum budget of $50 per year

- Membership sites for online courses. Minimum cost is about $80

- Email marketing platforms that require about $30 per month

- Etc.

Now, imagine working on all that and then nothing happens. You are not converting customers to sales yet the budget to set everything up was just unspeakable. On the other hand, if it works, do you see how everything is scattered? How are you going to collect data from the different sources and make an informed analysis? It is very hard to do so.

ClickFunnels cuts all that budget into one single fee of $97 per month and that's it. Everything you need is in one basket so you don't have to worry about creating a site and all the other supporting services that you will need to include. There are a lot of features in there but the main objective here is to make it easy for you to build a sales funnel from scratch.

Once you finish up on building, it's all about the one click down sells and upsells.

ClickFunnels Overview

Here is an overview of what you get out of ClickFunnels:

- Website template builder

- Sales funnel builder

- Opt-in and landing pages

- E-commerce platform

- Webinar pages

- Video launching

- Affiliate programs

- Countdown timers

- Email marketing programs

- A/B or split testing

- Integration with third-party platforms such as Shopify, MailChimp, and others

When you look at what this platform can provide for your business, one thing is clear here: ClickFunnels was built for entrepreneurs like you and me who don't know how to program or design to design pages in a sales funnel that will help you convert prospects into sales.

If you want an easy way to create a sales page, a landing page, an opt-in page among other pages you require, ClickFunnels does not need you to have prior knowledge of doing that. There are templates in the platform to help you set up and videos to show you how it's done. The templates are customizable since they provide you with areas to insert content and pictures that relate to your business in minutes.

With ClickFunnels, you don't have to worry about spending too much on developers and graphic designers since everything is there for you to pick. Over the years, there are other platforms to join like I mentioned in the beginning but there is one thing about them. Their complexity leads to slowness when building your funnel. Most of them are going too far with the drag and drop feature that is what makes everything slow. If you have joined a platform like Optimize Press 2.x, you know what I'm talking about.

ClickFunnels simplifies the building process by having to create the whole funnel under one roof and the one click upsells and downsells.

Another thing about ClickFunnels is that it helps you go from zero to hero. The platform is aware that you need more than a landing page and a sales page to help you convert your customers. That way, everything you need to automate your sales and make your dream a reality is included in one place.

At times, you might need a different system to make sales or introduce something new. In ClickFunnels, you only need a template that will allow you to change everything within the funnel. Do you want to connect your social media customers to your landing page or an opt-in to a webinar? Then all that goes to a thank you page? The complexity you need for your funnel to work can be handled by just using one funnel instead of having to spend on creating customized pages for the same output.

After doing all that, the emails you get are handled by the email program that allows you to send emails to your customers and address them using what they require. Most of the Sales Funnels platforms lack the email marketing module which is worse if you are looking on how to retarget your customers.

Last but not the least, ClickFunnels allows you to link third-party accounts and the payment processors directly to your funnel. That means you can link accounts that alert you when conversion occurs among other things that you would like to keep an eye on.

As I conclude the book, here is a summary of what ClickFunnels can do for you:

- It is easy to learn even when you don't have prior knowledge on how to set everything up

- It is one place for you to automate your sales funnel, email and social media marketing, and include an affiliate program.

- There is no limit to the amount of pages you need to create.

- You have a chance to perform A/B or split testing

- You can see how your business is performing by having the analysis on one dashboard

- Your pages respond well across all the devices form large computers to smartphones.

- They have a guide on everything you need to do

to set up and increase your conversion rate.

With that, do you want to build a successful sales funnel, using this guide and joining ClickFunnels is a guarantee that you will achieve what you are aspiring for in your business.

If you want to try Clickfunnels here is a free 14 day trial that you can have full access to
http://bit.ly/Omidsfreetrial

How to Build an Online Empire from Scratch

Before we begin I have a free gift for you from Russell Brunson - for those of you that don't know Russell Brunson is, he's the man that created ClickFunnels. In my opinion it's the best funnel website out there and it has also helped create the most millionaires. If you're reading this book then you want to be the best in your industry. This book will give you the play by play to have people PAYING you for your advice. I am able to give you his best selling book for free right down here. I only have a few copies left so please get them while you can. Just click this
http://bit.ly/giftfunnelbook

References

Rietkerk, R. (2019). ABM requires a new mindset, not just a technology overhaul. Retrieved from https://cxo.nl/management/97866-abm-requires-a-new-mindset--not-just-a-technology-overhaulPike, J. (2016). Account-based marketing (ABM): 10 things we learnt at this week's roundtable | B2B Marketing Account-based marketing: 10 things we learnt at this week's roundtable. Retrieved from https://www.b2bmarketing.net/en-gb/resources/articles/account-based-marketing-abm-10-things-we-learnt-weeks-roundtable

Burton, T. (2017). An 8-Step Account-Based Marketing Plan to Share with Your Boss. Retrieved from https://www.integrate.com/blog/8-step-account-based-marketing-plan

Velji, J. (2018). 5 Reasons You Need A Sales Funnel – Jamil Velji – Medium. Retrieved from https://medium.com/@jamilvelji/5-reasons-you-need-a-sales-funnel-64bf54481ee0 Davidoff, D. (2012). What Is A Strong Pipeline?. Retrieved from https://blog.imaginellc.com/what-is-a-strong-pipeline Ferenzi, K. (2019). Identifying Customers With A Target Market Analysis (Updated for 2019). Retrieved from https://www.bigcommerce.com/blog/target-market-analysis/#undefined Lazazzera, R. How To

Build Buyer Personas For Better Marketing. Retrieved from https://www.shopify.com/blog/15275657-how-to-build-buyer-personas-for-better-marketing

Mialki, S. (2018). The Lead Magnet: The Marketer's Best Way to Lure Prospects. Retrieved from https://instapage.com/blog/what-is-a-lead-magnetPatel, N. (2018). How to Create a High Converting Landing Page (12 Essential Elements). Retrieved from https://www.crazyegg.com/blog/landing-page-essentials/

Ciotti, G. (2019). Customer Service 101: A Guide to Providing Stand-Out Support Experiences. Retrieved from https://www.shopify.com/blog/customer-service#skills

Parkes, J. (2018). How to Craft a Call to Action That Converts | ClickFunnels - ClickFunnels. Retrieved from https://www.clickfunnels.com/blog/how-to-craft-call-to-action-that-converts/Jhajharia, R. (2018). 6 Unbeatable Benefits of Facebook Marketing Your Business Should Consider. Retrieved from https://www.digitalvidya.com/blog/benefits-of-facebook-marketing/Ference, A. (2017). 5 Paid Traffic Sources to Promote Your Website | Outbrain Blog. Retrieved from https://www.outbrain.com/blog/5-paid-traffic-sources/

Stych, J. What is Drip Marketing? The Complete Guide

to Drip Campaigns, Lifecycle Emails, and More. Retrieved from https://zapier.com/learn/email-marketing/drip-marketing-campaign/Bulygo, Z. (2019). How Being an Authority can Boost Your Online Sales. Retrieved from https://neilpatel.com/blog/being-an-authority/

Bendorf, B. 7 Ways to Convert Online Leads into Paying Customers (Infographic). Retrieved from https://www.ipaper.io/blog/ways-to-convert-online-leads